The Magazine of PICCADILLY PUBLISHING
The Home of Great Western Fiction!

Winter 2018 Issue

Cover Art:
Sergio Giovane

COME AHEAD AN' WELCOME!

When the subject of IPC's original *Western Magazine* was first raised by our Facebook followers, Mike Stotter and I realized that the magazine had, over the years, come to assume near-legendary status among its admirers. Neither of us saw that coming when we first took the idea to IPC Magazines way back in 1979. However, we ourselves had such great memories of acting as consultants on *Western Magazine* that we decided to try and recreate it with our very own PP-specific title. If your feedback is anything to go by, *Head West!* succeeded pretty well.

So ... what do we do for an encore? Well, how about no less than **FOUR** short western stories instead of last issue's three? How about an impressive **THIRTY** extra pages for your money—

in essence, more 'bang-bang-bang' for your buck?

Our contributors have labored long and hard to make this issue even better than the last, and your humble editor would like express his gratitude to each and every one of them – J. T. Edson and Rosica Colin Ltd., Ray Hogan and the Golden West Literary Agency, Neil Hunter (Mike Linaker), Tony Masero, Linda Pendleton, Mike Stotter (also for proofreading!) and Alfred Wallon. Now, read on ... and enjoy!

Ben Bridges
Suffolk

RIGHT ON TARGET!

PICCADILLY COWBOY SUPREMO
LAURENCE JAMES,
INTERVIEWED BY MIKE STOTTER

*I*n 1970 Laurence James became an editor at the paperback publishing house, New English Library. It was the beginning of a career that saw him become what he described as the country's "least known bestseller", writing (under pen-names) twelve to fourteen novels every year, 160 in total, which collectively sold more than 12m copies. He wrote a series of hell's angel novels as Mick Norman; Viking and Roman historical novels as Arthur Frazier, Andrew Quiller and Neil Langholm; science fiction under his own name; humorous 'confessions' as Jonathan May and Christopher Nolan; and romances as Mary Fraser. He produced dozens of Westerns, beginning in 1974 with the Apache *series (as William M James), a violent revenge story which ran over two dozen novels, as did the* Herne The Hunter *series for Corgi (written as John J McLaglen). This interview was conducted in November, 1978, when I was a bright-eyed, innocent fan-boy and was running* STEELE EDGE *(a fanzine that evolved from the* George G. Gilman Appreciation Society*).*

*****

MS: Going back to the beginning when you were an editor at NEL, did you ever think that you would become a full time writer?

LJ: No. It was down to people like Terry (Harknett) actually. It used to piss me off because we'd go and have lunch, a bottle of wine, some port and we used to have a nice time and then it would be half past two, three o'clock and Terry would say, "Well, better be going home now, don't want to be caught in the rush hour." And I would look at my watch and think, Christ, I've still got three-and-a-half hours to go. I thought, if he can do it, I can do it.

Laurence James, Mike Stotter, Terry Harknett

MS: Looking for the easy life...

LJ: It was partly that, but I wrote myself a letter when I quit NEL giving the reasons why, and if I ever found that writing wasn't going well I'd look at that letter and think, yeah, that's why I left. But

I've never had to because it's all gone so well. One of the reasons was the kids, being with the family. Because I used to leave the house at 7.30 and I would get home about 8 o'clock in the evening and I'd always have work with me. I got little kids then, very small and I literally never saw them in the week. I would see them on Saturdays, although I always had work then, I'd take it home, manuscripts and proofs to read. I just got fed up with it, I was there for three years and I would edit at the table and watch everybody get old. Faces lined and getting weary and I thought, 'God, do I want thirty-five years of that?' No, I didn't want thirty-five more years of that so I jacked it in, It wasn't really for the money. Money was purely incidental to it.

MS: What was the first book you ever wrote?

LJ: The first of the Hell's Angels: ANGELS FROM HELL for NEL. That was in early 1973 when I was just leaving NEL.

MS: How did that lead to the HELL'S ANGELS series?

LJ: What I did, I sent it through a friend, under a different name. I sent it into one of the other editors without telling anybody who it came from because it's a very difficult position at a publishers, when you want to write. Because if you write for someone else then it doesn't make you very popular and you get into trouble and equally, if you send a book into yourself then there's no way of knowing why it's being published or why it's being rejected, I mean, it might be rejected simply because you work there or might be bought because you work there and I didn't want to do that at all. So I sent it into a friend and deliberately kept out of it, I didn't want anything to do with it and just let it go through.

There was a very tight buying system at NEL. A book would come in and an editor would read it, and then it would have to go around to home sales manager, export sales manager, sales director, production manager, and back to the editor and then it would finally go to the finance director and managing director. So, it had to go through seven people before it was bought. So I figured that if it went through seven people and it all went through okay and it seemed to work, then I'd feel that I didn't abuse my position at all. So, it did do okay. And all the 'Angels' books sold well.

MS: How do you write your books – is it a case of sitting down at nine and work your way through a set period?

LJ: No, It's a set number of pages. What I do is, I know my delivery date, in the case of this book [then *Herne 11*] it's November 28th and so all my books are 200 quarto pages, double-spaced. They're always 199 to 201. I always hit it so, I figure it out by November 28th I've got to do 200 pages then I'd look how many working days I've got for that time

3

and how many days I might have off—like if it's the kids half term and we take them up to town to the pictures, so that's a dead day. Or if I've got engagements like you coming round, it only counts as half a day. And then I simply divide it up and it generally comes out at fourteen or fifteen pages a day, something like that. So I'd work it back to the first day, I'd do fourteen pages, the second day twenty-eight then right up to 200. It takes about three weeks to write a book. The women's series I'm doing for Sphere [*The Village*] is twice as long.

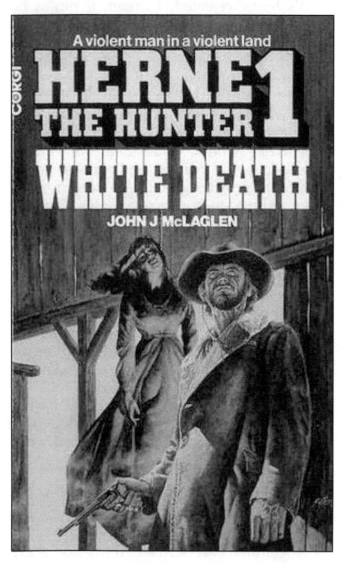

MS: When creating your characters such as Herne and Crow, do you visualize them as an actor, as Herne is something like Clint Eastwood?

LJ: Herne did start out something like him: It's quite often that you think of actors like Jack Palance or Lee Van Cleef or Clint Eastwood, people like that, and you tend to model the hero on them a little bit.

What you really want is what Hitchcock called the 'McGuffin'; you look for a gimmick for them. There's got to be something different for them. It's no good just having a hero who rides across the West killing people. You can't have a whole variety of gimmicks otherwise you'll turn up with a four foot, twenty-eight stone dwarf with a wooden leg. In Herne, for instance the gimmick was that he was old. 'Cos I wrote this with John Harvey, what we do is simply sit down together, like we're sitting here and we start from absolutely nothing and say right, 'What's he going to be like—how is he going to look, how is he going to dress, what sort of weapons is he going to use?'

We also wanted to try the idea of him having to drag a young girl around with him and in the end we decided that she was becoming superfluous and it wasn't working out the way we thought so we sent her off to Europe and then finally brought her back and she dies.

MS: Yeah, that's another question, why did you kill her off in Herne #7?

LJ: Well, she was becoming a bit of a pain in the ass, really. She wasn't doing an awful lot. We'd done the things with her that we wanted to do, because when you start a series, you never know how long it is going to run and we figured with Herne that it'd run until the revenge bit was over. That was for three books, and that I would leave Herne and the girl completely on their own. I thought that it would be nice having them together, something like PAPER MOON. It never kind of really worked—whether to sleep with her or not, I mean. It was quite strongly referred through her dying; she says she wishes that he had. But in the end we thought that we might as well kill her off. It was a smashing weepy scene. I loved that, it was like when his Louise died.

MS: Would you describe your characters as heroes or anti-heroes?

LJ: Oh, they're heroes.

MS: Well-defined heroes—do they always win in the end?

LJ: Well, Dylan said that there's no success like failure and failure's no success at all. I mean that's what the heroes are like. All my heroes are flawed. They are all losers in a way as they never actually get anything positive. None of them actually becomes rich, none of them becomes happy. They are something like a blunt instrument moving through the West.

What is it that they say in THE MAGNIFICENT SEVEN? At the end, the old man says something like: "You're like the wind that moves through and cleans the land." That's what the heroes are really like, they move through and they never get involved. Like at the ending of THE SEARCHERS where John Wayne comes up to the door and they take the girl inside and everybody' a happy and he's ruined his life searching for this girl. And in the end he just turns around

and walks away again because a Western hero cannot get involved.

There's no such thing as a happy, rich Western hero. Never. They can't be. They get to be men alone. Like Edge. Like Herne, they've got to keep moving on. Generally as they leave things better than they found them, they've got to be heroes.

MS: Would you ever consider, under the name of John J. McLaglen doing a book featuring Whitey Coburn, set before when he and Herne were in their heydays?

LJ: Number #9 is the flashback one, isn't it?

MS: Yeah, that's MASSACRE!

LJ: We might flashback, because we've dropped hints here and there of things that Herne did when he rode with Cody on the Pony Express. This one here's a reference of when he knew Jesse James. There are various things we might go back again and do another flashback one. At the moment we are thinking of selling two more to Corgi and probably one of those might be a flashback one with Billy the Kid, because it seemed to work well, quite nice in fact. I like Whitey Coburn.

MS: Yeah he's a brilliant character. Did you base him on anyone?

LJ: Several of my books have had an albino in them. I truly don't know why—I like the idea of paleness and white hair. Dramatic.

MS: I think the good thing about Herne is that he is an ageing gunfighter who is past his heyday and he's got a good code of honor.

LJ: Yes, this is in fact in the book I am writing now, number 11. He has this sort of confrontation with this kid who he thinks is out to kill him and he is constantly coming up against the punks who have heard about Herne the Hunter who is coming out of retirement and they go after him. This kid is absolutely really nothing. We never even know what his name is and Herne doesn't care anything about him. Has nothing really but contempt and he knows he has set out to kill him and they are facing each other and the sheriff tries to interfere and the kid says, "You keep out of this, you don't know what's going on between the old man and me."

It is at that moment that Herne, for the only time, has a bit of respect for the kid because there is this kind of code between them and the sheriff (the outsider) doesn't understand and it is just between the two of them. When the kid dies and is buried on the grave marker it just has the day and the month and year and it says, "He was a kid of 18 and not as fast ae he thought he was," and that's all it says.

MS: Is there one book you would like to write regardless of being commissioned, just the one thing every author is looking for in life—the multi-million pound bestseller, or are you just content on writing series?

LJ : It's a difficult question, but I've got a lot of ideas. Ideas for very uncommercial books that sometime I might write just because I want to write them. It depends on the time. I'm like Terry (Harknett), we are very similar in some

ways to our attitude in writing. We regard it as a professional job. If I've got the time and I feel I can do it I will write anything for anybody and I would like to write for film or T.V. If I could have the time and the money was worth it, but it's very difficult to set out to write blockbusting best-sellers. It can be done, you can manufacture it.

MS: Do you have that series 'The Old West' from TimeLife, and do you use them a lot in your research?

LJ: I've got about four of them. I've got 'THE GUNFIGHTERS', 'THE INDIANS' and 'THE EXPRESSMEN.' I don't collect all of them as a series as some of them are specialized. I don't actually use them a lot for research. The single book I use most in my research is 'BOOTHROYD'S—THE HANDGUN' which is a great fat hardback, it's out of print now, but it's a superb book on handguns. It's got photographs, exploded drawings—a terrific amount of information. And I use it a hell of a lot.

MS: Like some other writers, do you have a collection of replica guns?

L.J: I've got a Colt .45, a Mauser, the Winchester, the Luger—that's the Navy Parabellum. The problem is that you can't play with them, 'cos they break.

MS: I don't know. I have a good time with mine.

LJ: The hammer on the Colt keeps breaking all the time. I've got through three hammers. They're not really intended to be played with and I tend to play with them quite a lot. Also the Luger jams.

MS: Do you find, say using the Colt—is it the Army or the Navy one?

LJ: The Peacemaker.

MS: Well, do you use what you discover when playing with them, as in The Gunslinger series—'the triple click of the Colt...'?

LJ : Yes—I can't get away from that triple click actually. I use it quite a lot. Like Terry and the word 'power'. They are useful then. I remember once when I was doing one of the Norman-Saxon series, WOLFSHEAD, I think, which I did with Ken Bulmer., and I got this scene where this Norman sergeant was protecting this woman from behind, against this crowd of outlaws. He was holding them off with his sword, and she, in fact, was the Lady of the Manor, and when it becomes obvious to him that they are going to beat him down and kill him, he decides that he must save her from a fate worse than death. So he cuts her throat before they kill him. It was a very difficult thing to do, physically. Normally, I use Liz for this sort of thing (use the wife as props) and I had to do this myself this one time. I have several knives and things, I was standing in my room, pulling it across my throat trying to

work it out. I suddenly looked up, the house was being decorated, and the painter outside was staring through the window looking horrified at the sight of this man apparently making several unsuccessful attempts to cut his own throat!

MS: Do you do that sort of thing often?

LJ: For action scenes, I do. I sort of get into it, it's quite useful. I don't use my wife for the naughty bits.

MS: When you write a Western and you have just been reading a SF book, does it influence you at all, like Angus says he is very influenced by what he has read beforehand?

LJ: No. I am influenced by what I am reading at the time and writing for pleasure can be influenced. That is why, whatever I am writing, I make sure that if I am doing an ordinary reading for pleasure I won't read anything that it is at all connected with it. What is disastrous in some ways and good in others, is to watch a Western film when you are writing a Western. Because you tend to find that you get some very good lines that you can work in. That's true of music. You know that all of us, particularly Angus and I and I think John, use lines from songs and work in song references. In fact, when I read a book a year later I can always tell what I have been playing on the jukebox or record player because the lines come into it, you can't keep it away.

MS: How do you relax when you are not writing? Do you garden?

LJ: No. Well, I mow the lawn. Liz is really in charge of the garden. We've got a big lawn, about an acre and it takes time in the summer. And I'm quite involved in the local boys' football team: The Roydon Rangers; David plays for the under elevens and Matthew is going to play for the under 10s, though he is only six. And Cathy's a sixer in the Brownies. I'm very much a family man, not very interesting.

Before we got married, fifteen years ago, we used to go to the pictures an awful lot. We used to go two or three times a week to the National Film Theatre but when the kids came it was very difficult. We virtually stopped going to the pictures for about nine years, but we have just discovered the Harlow Playhouse which is a regional film theatre. It's very convenient for us and it it's okay to get a babysitter and we've started going to the pictures again a lot because they show films like 'Midnight Cowboy', 'Easy Rider', 'Woodstock', 'Network'. The kind of films you really want to see but we missed because we were not going then.

MS: I know you have you've visited the States twice now. Do you feel that you can write about the West with more confidence?

LJ: Yes. It's a very difficult thing to define because it's not a very specific thing. What you can do is actually *feel* it better. I've been on the Custer Battlefield at Little Big Horn for instance, and that gives you something that no book or film could ever give. It gives you the feeling of what it was like.

You can stand there, halfway up the hill and look down on the river, look across the Reno-Benteen site on your left and behind you is where they nearly made it. And you can see these white markers dotting the hills because it's almost exactly as it was. You think, "Christ, you can see why they didn't make it," and it's there. It's the same down in the South-West with the heat. All these corny things like what the rocks really look like, what hot earth feels like in your hands, when it's like in the shade and that kind of thing.

MS: It's that sort of thing gives you authenticity ...

LJ: I think it's a help. It's not essential because Terry and I had both written a lot of Westerns before either of us went over there. We had two seven weeks holidays there and covered a lot of miles and it was very nice.

MS: What is it like co-writing the Herne series with John? Do you read each other's books?

LJ: Yes, the co-writing is quite easy providing it's someone you can rely on and trust their style to be more or less like yours. I often wonder actually how much other people can tell that it's co-written, whether the join shows. To us, it's obvious. I can tell my style against John's or Angus's or Terry's but I wonder how much other people can tell.

MS: I couldn't really tell the join with the Cade series because Terry wrote one to three and then Angus took over, they were so similar.

LJ: Angus is so good at adapting his style, very good indeed, but I think with Herne we had slight problems around about numbers four and five. Things didn't work out well for a couple of books but then we clicked and it got better and now it's all okay.

MS: You can usually tell when you are taking over a book because sex keeps on creeping in.

LJ: No sex at all in my Westerns!

MS: What?

LJ: No sex at all. A little bit. I don't have great rape scenes like Terry does. He's the King of Rape. If ever you have a blonde lady in one of Terry's books it's absolutely a million to one that she's going to be raped before the book is out.

MS: When readers pick up a Western do you think they go for it because of the storyline or for its violent contents, for which you are well known for?

LJ: I really don't know. It's very difficult, say 50,000 people buy Herne, I might ever met two or three of them. It's a fair bet that a lot of them will be fairly intelligent people like you.

MS: Do you think that the covers to your books play an important part in selling them?

LJ: Yeah, they must do. Bearing in mind that I'm an ex-paperback editor you get very cynical. When you work for a paperback house you get to wonder if you're selling books or cans of baked beans. It's just a question of if you put a really eye-catching label on the baked beans or not, if the one brand will sell better than another or if it's better advertised.

MS: Do you have a favorite artist?

LJ: I like Dick Clifton Dey's work. I mean it's invidious to mention him because most of the others I've liked as well, Bruce Pennington on the science fiction works, he did some smashing covers for me. I like Backhouse and Collingwood. The big thing about Dick's covers was that they were really good. They were lively, lots of stuff going on and they were interesting covers; you kind of worked out what the book was about just by looking at the cover. There's so much thought in them. I think that nowadays, too many people think, "Oh, it's another Edge." I think it's a shame.

I work quite closely with the artist on a lot of them. With Chris Collingwood particularly because he's doing the covers on Crow. He'll ring me up and say "I've got to do two more covers for Herne, when are they set, what time of year is it, is there anything particular you want in them?" There's been occasions where we've actually gone the other way around. As the Herne been published with the table being knocked over during a fight—or is that the next one: number 10? Must be, because on that one we only had a loose synopsis on it and Chris Collingwood was saying what did I want in it and I'd said that we're quite free, is there anything you'd like to put on it? You put it on the cover and we'll put it in the book. He said that he'd always wanted to do a gunfight in a saloon with a table being knocked over, things like that and so he did it. And because it was sufficiently early, we were able to get a copy of it, in fact John Harvey wrote it and John was able to put the scene into the book with the characters looking as they actually do. It sometimes works that way.

It worked on one of the SF covers, I was talking to Bruce Pennington and sometimes, when I sell to publishers, I don't give them a synopsis at all. I mean, once a series is I might just say, "Do you want to buy two more Hernes or whatever," but in this case for the SIMON RACK series, I'd got no idea what it was going to be about at all, so I said to Pennington, "What would you like to do on a cover?" He said that he's always liked the idea of people floating in transparent globes. I said, "Yeah. That ought to be good, so all right. Do that on the cover and I'll fit it in." It worked out okay.

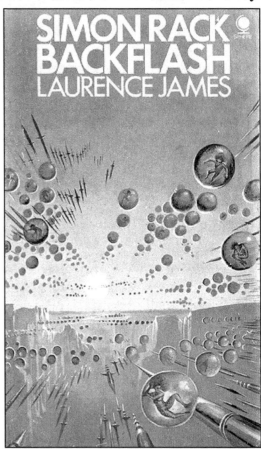

MS: What does your family think of your writing?

LJ: The kids are too young to read my stuff anyway. They're ten, eight and six at the moment. They're very blasé about it actually. I'm a writer like anyone else say, is a bus conductor. There's absolutely no difference to them. I mean it is just a job, that's all it is to me. Just a job. My wife Liz, she reads some of the stuff, she's read the woman's series that I'm doing, she's read quite a lot of the earlier books. She read the JOURNALS OF... But basically, she's not into Westerns really. Which is fair enough; she likes Western movies. Again, as far as she is concerned it's another job. It pays the mortgage.

MS: A corny question: Where do you get your ideas for your books. Do they just come up?

LJ: When people know that you're a writer, the one question you're always asked is: "Where do you get your ideas from?" and I was talking to Fred Nolan about it, and he said, "Yes, Laurence, When people do that, do what I do. Say there's this book published in 1938 by the University of Pennsylvania Press, when you become a writer you're sworn to secrecy, you're not supposed to tell anybody about this. It's like the Masonic secret. But there is this book published. It's 1100 pages long and it contains 6,350 plots for books and when you tell people about this, they'll go, 'Ahh, that's how you do it!' Then they're much happier then you say that you just make them up, because they don't believe it. I've done that and people do go, "Ahh, so that's how you do it!"

They just come, books to a certain extent write themselves. Because characters take over, things never quite go the way you intend them to go. There's been characters in series (Whitey Coburn for instance) like Sheriff Nolan who you suddenly get interested in and say, "Hey, they're good characters." They're characters you think that are going to start off as being evil and in fact, become sympathetic with. Or the other way around, characters you think are going to be nice people you suddenly think, "Christ, they're pretty shitty really, aren't they?" So you write them in and do it that way.

MS: Talking of characters—do you keep an information sheet?

LJ: I've got a rough character sheet, yeah. In this respect the most difficult thing has been this woman's series from that point of view. It's a kind of up market soap-opera in a way. You don't do any research on it before hand, that way it's a reverse of the usual book. Like say, if I'm doing a war series, I'll spend two or three days getting all my research material together—the cockpit layout of a Messerschmitt, the muzzle velocity of this and that. But with this particular series I had to do it as I went along— keeping copious notes. Like how many sugars Mrs. So and So takes, because the next time she appears she has got to have the same amount of lumps. And where they live, what color their bedroom carpet is, what school their second child goes to. I've done three of those so far and something like sixty pages of notes, all cross-referenced. I've got five maps—again important in that sort of series. You've got to know where everything is; I know that the post office is directly opposite the greengrocers, that sort of information has got to be right in every book. It's quite difficult in that series.

MS: It's the same with the Western characters, they are bound to bump into one another sooner or later, aren't they?

LJ: That's already started. I don't know if it's Terry, but we've started putting in occasional references. Caleb Thorn and Crow have cameo appearances in the Herne I'm writing at the moment, not physically appearing but ... 'It reminded him of something that he'd been told once, what was it? Was it that Cavalry officer Caleb, Caleb Thorn? Or was it that busted man from the battle of the Little Big Horn, Crow?' that kind of thing. Or someone'll be riding along and say that there's been no Apache trouble since that Cuchilo Oro vanished. We do that kind of thing a lot. What Terry and I would like to do at some point, is to write a joint Edge-Herne book, I said that I wouldn't do it until Herne had become really established and successful. Because I wasn't prepared to ride on the back of Edge, But I mean, Herne seems to be doing quite well at the moment.

MS: What sort of sales figures has it?

LJ: They're doing 50's (50,000) upwards, which is quite nice. They're buying more and they're getting a good response from the people at Bookwise, the distributors. I think that maybe in a year or so we'll think about it. If I can get Herne up to, say fifteen or eighteen, then one can assume that it is reasonably well established then and I won't be riding on his back. But the problem will come with the publishers. Seeing that they are different, who would publish it? Would they both do it? It could be done.

MS: It'll be historical.

LJ: It would be. The way we thought of doing it would be that we'd write alternate chapters. Say a ten chapter book, we'd have to plot it out carefully. With Terry's chapter it would have Edge as the hero and Herne with him and in my chapter have Herne move to the center of the stage.

MS: Mind you, they're both getting old now. Edge is what, forty-ish?

LJ: Yeah, Herne is forty-one, I think. Which, in real terms, was quite an old man. Not many of them made it to be very old.

MS: Have you got a least favorite novel you've written?

LJ: No. They're all brilliant. They're absolutely superb.

MS: Well, is there one that's not as outstanding as the rest?

LJ: It's funny when you write them—we all feel this as writers – when you are doing it there are times when you are not happy and think it wasn't as good as it might have been. Then you sub next day, or whenever it might be. I generally sub the next day, and there are times when you think, "Well, it's okay." But when you read the proofs (the next step) it gets better and you think: "Yeah, that's really okay." And when you get the finished book, you think, "That's amazingly brilliant. God, that's terrific," Because I've just got the proofs to ARIZONA BLOODLINE and that's really good, got some good things in it. Lots of nice little jokes and things, good action stuff as well.

MS: Who are your favorite authors ... apart from yourself.

LJ: That would be invidious. I'm forced to mention Terry, Angus, John Harvey and Fred Nolan—whether they are not.

MS: Do you read their books?

LJ: We dip into each other's works. We have a lot of trouble with titles. I don't know if Terry has mentioned this, because we are writing a lot of Westerns. Terry writes on his own; Angus writes on his own and with me and with John, John writes on his own and with me and with Angus; I write on my own and with Angus and with John. One of the most difficult things in writing a book is thinking up a name for your character which is incredibly difficult.

MS: I've noticed that they've become short and sharp: Edge, Crow, Steele ...

LJ: Crow, in fact, came from Patrick Janson Smith, Editor at Corgi—he thought it up. It's a good name. Pen-names are difficult to think up as well. Surprisingly difficult. People who aren't writers wouldn't think about it but it's very difficult to come up with a good pen-name.

MS: Names such as L. J. Coburn is Laurence James and add the Coburn, isn't it?

LJ: Right, and John J. McLaglen is John Ford and Victor McLaglen—that's where that came from. Klaus Netzen in the KILLERS series was simply because I wanted a German name.

MS: I think he appears in a Herne adventure.

LJ: That's right, he does. Christ, they keep cropping up. It's amazing how many cross-indexed and cross-references there are to friends, other people's names like this. Like Trooper Stotter and Trooper Whitehead appear in Crow # 1. Little cameo bits like that. Angus Wells appears as a town in one occasion; 'They rode into Angus Wells...' He was a superb creation once, in one of the *Confession* books, he was a lady called Angustura Wells. I thought Angustura was terrific.

MS: You always turn up as a barkeep or similar.

LJ: Yeah, I always get crappy roles. I writer I know (Gordon Newman) who did that television series 'Law and Order', put me in and I was in that actually by name. He also wanted me to play a part in it because they were filming in Dublin and they wanted this guy who was to come in and bugger this informer in a cell. I didn't fancy it really. But he's put me in some of his books and he appears in some of mine. He gives me rotten parts. Once I appeared as homosexual twins named Laurence and James. Which, I thought, was a bit mean.

MS: Angus is always getting his knees blown off or being splattered across the room.

LJ: It's the same with book dedications, we quite often find cross-dedications, One of the Confessions book is dedicated: 'This is to Uncle Angus who rides tall in the saddle, but you'd ride tall in the saddle if you had piles like Uncle Angus!' It's that kind of thing that makes it all worthwhile—you can amuse yourself whilst doing it as well, you see.

MS: When writing your Western series, do you find it difficult to think up new situations for them?

LJ: No, not yet. I generally don't see any problem at all in plotting or any danger of running out of ideas.

MS: It seems that many series all start off with the revenge theme.

LJ: Yes. You have your basic revenge motive, which is a good one. There is a revenge motive in Crow to start it off.

MS. Plus dishonor from the Cavalry.

LJ: That's right. There is revenge in all of them because I think it is the single strongest motive. I don't think you have basically got a guy who has become a bounty hunter because he wants to become a bounty hunter, or a gunman simply because he enjoys it. There's always some sort of terrible trauma in his past life that made him decide he would like to do it.

MS: Do you get much fan-mail?

LJ: I did on the *Confessions*. Actually, I solicited it. I had literally hundreds of letters, amazing letters, and photographs. Offers ... you wouldn't believe.

MS: Any mail for Westerns?

LJ: No, virtually none. I think people often write when they think they have caught you out on a mistake. So far I don't think we have any particular mistakes in Westerns.

MS: Do you see the Western fiction market reaching saturation point?

LJ: I don't know. We are doing our bit to flood it between us I think that any publisher that buys a Western series that isn't written by Terry or John or Fred or Angus or me is taking a bit of a chance. Most of our series have been pretty successful whereas I think some of the others haven't done so well. Goodness knows how many Western series we are doing at the moment. We must have ten going altogether! It is amazing that they all sell, Between us we are writing fifty odd books a year of which, over half are Westerns.

MS: Finally, what advice would you give for would-be writers?

LJ: Just do it. There's absolutely no other advice to give. Type on one side of the paper, double-space it, number every page, make sure your name's on it and your address, make sure you put a note somewhere of how long the book is (rough word count). It's that kind of think that would guarantee that a publisher would at least look at it. 'Cos if you send it in, generally speaking, and it's not reasonably presented and not fairly legible, people aren't going to bother. Because what publishers want are authors that are fairly professional in their attitude. If you are sloppy and careless, publishers just won't bother with it.

It is fairly difficult to give advice about writing, again, as a publisher it is something you get cynical about. I was buying something like 150-200 books a year at NEL and out of about every 100 books I bought, I would have thought that probably twenty-five were commissioned originals, which meant me going to a specific author, say Terry, and say would you do a book on whatever? I would have thought that the other seventy odd, probably sixty-five would have come from other publishers, about five would come from agents and one would be an unsolicited manuscript.

There is an astronomical amount of people who think that they can write and the trouble is that people are so un-self-critical and by the nature of life and social conventions, if they give their manuscript to a friend or relative to read, it's a racing certainty that they say, "It's very good ... It's smashing" and unfortunately, in real terms they are totally misinformed and they're told lies.

Again, that is something I would never do, I'd never read a manuscript for anybody. One thing I've learnt in publishing is when someone says, "Will you read this and I want your honest opinion," in fact, what they want you to say is, "Tell me how good it is." And unfortunately, it almost always isn't.

That's why people complain about publishers, saying, "Why don't they send proper rejection slips explaining what's wrong with it?"

The reason is with a proportion of people, maybe with ten per cent of the rejection slips if you wrote and told them what you thought of it, you would get involved with an amazing stream of correspondence.

They'll come to the office and they'll keep re-writing it and sending it in again, and if you rejected it, they'd get annoyed saying, "Well I did what you said to do. I changed all the dialogue." And unfortunately, that's how it works.

Photos © Mike Stotter

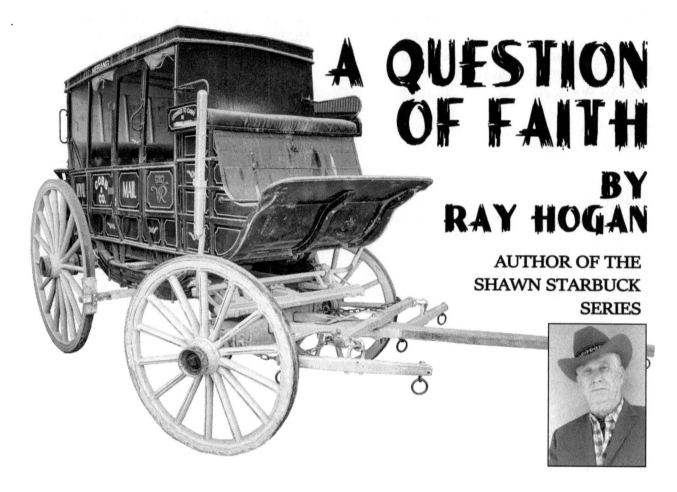

A QUESTION OF FAITH

BY RAY HOGAN

AUTHOR OF THE SHAWN STARBUCK SERIES

It was the time of war, the bloody, senseless conflict of ideologies now mercifully reeling toward its finish. New Mexico, having had its brief fling with shot and shell, hung suspended in neglected vacuum aware of the struggle only by reports from far distant battlefields or the occasional glimpse of a blue-uniformed patrol riding a remote trail. Mid July and the afternoon heat lay across the broad plains and choppy hills in a blistering haze. Overhead the sky was cobalt steel, and along its edges cloud mountains piled up in masses of jumbled, cotton batting to rim a breathlessly hot world in which nothing moved but vagrant dust-devils and the stagecoach bound for Rinconada.

Driver Luke Colegrove, the leather ribbons laced between his fingers sawing his arms back and forth as the double span of lathered blacks pressed against the harness, flung a sideward glance to Ed Drummond that day beside him on the box.

"Anything?"

Drummond again swept the savage terrain with his keen scrutiny. He shook his head, mopped at the sweat oozing freely from his weathered face. "Nope ... nothin'." He waited a minute as the coach slowed around a curve, rocked precariously, righted itself, and plunged on. "You figure Cannon knowed what he was talkin' about? Never heard of Confederate guerrillas being this far west before."

Colegrove, an acid little man with hawk-like features and a straggling yellow mustache, said: "He knowed. Them guerrillas been stopping coaches all over the country, hunting them two women."

Drummond digested that in silence. Then: "Figure to tell the passengers? Bound to throw a powerful scare into them."

"They got a right to know. We get to Cook's, I'll speak my piece. You do some talking to that hostler. See if he's seen any signs of them. Was ten, maybe twelve in the bunch. Cannon wasn't for sure."

Thirty minutes later they rushed into Cook's Station, rolling the dust ahead of them in a great, yellow boil, and came to a sliding stop. The hostler trotted up with fresh horses and immediately began to make his change. Drummond, not relinquishing his rifle, turned to him. Luke Colegrove swung down, yanked open the coach door.

"Ten minutes, folks. Stretch your legs and get yourself a swallow of water." He wheeled away, entered the low-roofed, adobe hut where further refreshments were to be had.

The passengers began to crawl stiffly from the cramped confines of the stage into the glaring sunlight. First, Mrs. Russell, a plump, gray woman, middle-aged and the wife of a territorial delegate. Next came her daughter, just turned seventeen. She was pretty, blue-eyed, and filling out her stylishly cut traveling suit to perfection. On their way to visit relatives in Silver City, it was said.

The third fare was a portly cattleman from Las Vegas, Armstrong by name. He was prone to much dozing and, when awake, fiddled constantly with a gold toothpick attached to a thin chain issuing from the top buttonhole of his checkered vest. He was a man who moved deliberately and with care, his ponderous bulk pressing the springs of the coach to basic level as he shifted to one side and emerged through the door.

The fourth fare was Dave Kirby, young, barely in his twenties in fact, with a rashness upon his features, a caged wildness glowing in his eyes. Handcuffs linked his wrists, and these glinted as sunlight touched the nickeled metal. His journey would end at Rinconada where he would stand trial for murder. He halted, leaned against the rear wheel of the vehicle in studied insolence as he awaited the tall lawman who followed close on his heels.

He was John Prince, marshal of Springville, in the process of delivering a prisoner. Lean of face, lank of body, a heavy personal trouble now lay upon him like a shroud, turning him taciturn and cold, and, when he placed his narrow glance on Dave Kirby, fresh anger stirred within him for he knew the outlaw was aware of that trouble. Kirby had been present during that hour before the stage departed Springville. He had witnessed the stormy scene, heard the bitter words that had passed between the tall lawman and his wife, Kate. Jealousy in a man is a pitiless scourge, forcing the worst to the surface—and the soul of John Prince had been laid bare before the outlaw.

Armstrong paused, stretched, yawned. The two women looked about uncertainly. Kirby caught the eye of the younger, smiled, his expression suddenly boyish.

"Water's inside, ma'am," he said, and nodded at the hut.

The girl thanked him and, with her mother, moved toward the sagging struc-

ture. At that moment Colegrove appeared, wiping at his mouth with the back of a hand. He glanced at Drummond, still in conversation with the hostler, halted, brushed his sweat-stained hat to the back of his head.

John Prince swore softly under his breath. He'd hoped to deliver Kirby and return quickly to Springville. The thought of Kate alone—with time on her hands—with Wilson Coyle subtly pressing his flattery and attentions upon her gouged into him

like a saw-edged blade. He had not wanted to make the trip to Rinconada in the first place, but there'd been no choice. Now it appeared something was coming up that would keep him away even longer.

Resentment sharpened his tone. "Now, why ... ?"

"Guerrillas," Colegrove spat. "Maybe part of Quantrell's bunch. Been stopping stages on this road last few days."

"Quantrell?" Armstrong echoed in frank disbelief. "This far west?"

The old driver shrugged. "Confederate

guerrillas been spotted east of here. And in Texas. Just about everywhere, in fact."

There was a lengthy silence in the streaming sunlight broken only by the rattle of harness metal as the hostler worked at his chore.

John Prince said: "You carrying a money shipment?"

Colegrove wagged his head. "Only a smidgen of mail."

"Then why," Mrs. Russell said, dabbing at the patches of sweat on her face with a lace handkerchief, "would they want to bother us?"

Colegrove looked directly at the woman, his beaten features solemn. "Reckon it's you they're wanting, ma'am. You and your daughter."

Mrs. Russell caught at her breath. The handkerchief went to her lips to stifle a cry. Instantly Martha placed her arm around the older woman's shoulders. She stared at Colegrove.

"Why ... why us?"

"Your daddy's a big man in this here country. Was I guessing, I'd say they figured to hold you for ransom."

"Maybe," Armstrong said. "Heard tell how Confederate guerrillas are always pulling raids to get women for ..."

"Forget it," Prince snapped. He swung his angry, impatient attention to the stagecoach driver. "Why the hell didn't you say something about this back at the fort? Could've asked for a cavalry escort."

Colegrove spat into the dust. "Didn't know about it. Just got the word at the last stop. Anyway," he added, glancing over the party, "I expect there's enough of us to give them an argument, if they try stopping us."

Prince allowed his jaundiced gaze to travel over the group. Enough—hell! Two women, an outlaw a man couldn't trust beyond arm's length, and a fat cow-nurse who'd likely curl up on the floor at the first shot. Only Drummond, the shotgun rider,

18

might be relied upon for help—and, if the raiders were smart, they'd shoot him off the box at the start. Far as Colegrove was concerned, he could be counted out of it; he'd have his hands full with the team.

Mrs. Russell began to weep raggedly. Martha drew her closer, patting her on the arm gently.

Colegrove bit off a fresh chew of tobacco. "Right sorry I had to tell you about this, but I figured you ought to know. Now, everybody get aboard. Let's get moving."

Drummond came up at that point. "Pete says he ain't seen nobody around that maybe looks like guerrillas. Says he seen smoke west of here this mornin'."

Colegrove thought for a moment. "Could've been pilgrims. Or maybe 'Paches," he said, and started for the coach.

Armstrong hurried into the hut for his drink. The women turned back, Mrs. Russell supported by her daughter. Dave Kirby stepped up quickly to assist, handing first the older woman and then Martha into the heat-trapped interior of the vehicle. Prince saw the girl touch the outlaw with her glance, expressing her thanks, and the thought—*Why will a woman always go for this kind?*—passed through his head. Shrugging then, he followed Kirby into the coach, settled himself on the forward seat next to the outlaw. A moment later Armstrong, puffing from the short sprint, took his place on the rear bench.

Colegrove shouted to the team, and they lunged forward, yanking the stage into forward motion with a violent rocking. Dust at once lifted between the opposed seats, began to rise and fall in a powdery cloud as the heat-charged air surged through the enclosure. In the road's deep ruts the coach crackled and popped and groaned from stress, those sounds blending gradually with Luke Colegrove's strident shouting.

Talk, desultory at best prior to the halt at Cook's Station, was now a dead issue, each passenger wrapped deeply in his own thoughts. John Prince was thinking of the past, of the seven years of married life with Kate who had grown more beautiful as time went by. Once he had been proud of

her beauty, was vaguely complimented that she was the target for other men's eyes. Now it was a red-hot iron searing through his chest. How had that come to be? When had it begun?

Somewhere, sometime ... One day Kate and he were as any married couple, happy, content, insofar as means permitted, loving in a comfortable, satisfying way, and then the next there had been change. Their status had not altered, yet there was a difference between them, a sullen anger, a wariness and suspicion that fattened on the hours while they were apart.

Wilson Coyle, that old friend of bygone years, had much to do with it, Prince was sure. Not that he knew anything with certainty, it was simply—well, the way things looked, sounded—and in his profession he had learned to have little faith in mankind, and always expect the worst.

The heat increased. Armstrong removed his coat and hung it across the window sill, unbuttoned his straining vest. Mrs. Russell improvised a fan with her purse, waved persistently at her flushed face. She had recovered her composure, no longer wept but sat now perfectly quiet, her pale features frozen. Beside her Martha studied her fingertips, eyes downcast, dark lashes resting upon her cheeks. Once she looked up, placed her attention on John Prince.

"Will we get help at the next stop?"

"Not this side of Silver City," he snapped, the sharpness of his voice betraying the turmoil raging within him.

The girl colored, glanced away, chastened by his abruptness.

"Don't you mind the marshal none, ma'am," Kirby said in a light, mocking tone. "He plain don't like nobody. Not even hisself."

Prince shifted his bitter glance to the outlaw, but there was no change in his expression. He shrugged as the coach slammed on down the rutted road. Let the bastard talk. Let him run off at the mouth ... his days were numbered. And far as he personally was concerned, it didn't matter what others thought. The whole human race could go to hell.

The shouts of Luke Colegrove lifted, and the coach began to pitch and sway with greater intensity. Armstrong thrust his head through the window, made his absent survey and murmured—"Coming into the hills."—and settled back. Prince glanced through the opening, saw the flat country swelling gradually into definite knolls that grew larger in the distance.

Outside the hard running of the horses was a steady drumming. The iron tires of the wheels screamed through the loose sand, clanged against rock, and the dust was an enveloping cloud racing with the coach. Luke's yells had become a constant sound, lashing at the horses as they began to climb a long grade. Frowning red buttes closed in on either side, and suddenly they were in a narrow channel.

Good place for an ambush, John Prince thought, and that induced him to sweep back the skirt of his coat, make his pistol more easily available. Martha Russell noted that and laid her questioning glance upon him. He

merely shook his head, turned away.

The coach began to slow as the drag of the grade took its toll on the horses' speed. Colegrove's yells increased, well interspersed with profanity, but they were drawing near a crest as the diminishing height of the buttes indicated.

Suddenly they were on the summit, wheeling around a sharp bend and picking up speed. Unexpectedly they began to slow. Ed Drummond shouted something unintelligible. Immediately following there came the sharp, spiteful crack of his rifle. Prince stiffened, drew his weapon, and

twisted about to peer through the window. A dozen yards or so ahead a scatter of riders milled about on the road, were blocking their passage.

"I'm going through 'em," Luke Colegrove yelled, and began to ply the whip. "Hang on!"

Prince threw a quick glance to Armstrong, was surprised to see the big man draw his long-barreled pistol, rest it upon the window sill. He looked then to the girl.

"Down on the floor ... quick!"

She obeyed instantly. The lawman motioned Kirby to her vacated spot. The outlaw complied hastily, and, when it was done, the girl was below them, protected by their legs, while Mrs. Russell was sandwiched securely between Armstrong on one side, Dave Kirby on the other. Prince thus had the rear seat to himself, enabling him to slide back and forth and watch both sides of the road.

Ed Drummond's rifle cracked again, and then became a continuing hammering as answering shots came from the road. The coach began to sway and reel, and dust became a choking, oppressive factor in breathing. Prince cast a calculating look at Mrs. Russell. She would be breaking down, going to pieces any moment now, and they'd have more problems. He ordered Kirby to look after her, keep her out of the way.

Reaching inside his coat he drew a second pistol, the one he'd taken off Dave Kirby and now evidence in the pending case, laid it on the seat. From a pocket he obtained a bandanna into which a handful of spare cartridges had been placed, dropped them beside Kirby's gun.

"Could give you a hand," the outlaw said, ducking his head at the weapon.

Prince shrugged. "No, thanks."

"My neck, too," Kirby said.

"But my responsibility," the lawman replied, and closed the subject.

Drummond's firing continued, and now Armstrong began to lay down his shots as they drew abreast the raiders. The acrid smell of powder smoke at once filled the coach, overriding the dust, and Colegrove's shouts began to mingle with others coming from the road. Bullets began to thud into the coach, dimpling the paneling. Armstrong jumped when one splintered the wood above his head.

They reeled through the cluster of waiting riders, two of which were falling slowly from their saddles. A dark, whiskered man wearing a faded forage cap swerved in close, mouth open in a wild yell. Prince took deliberate aim, pressed off his shot. The man jolted, wilted, fell. Ed Drummond's rifle had gone silent, and, wondering about it, the lawman looked back. The guard was a crumpled bundle of dusty clothing in the road.

Prince swore silently. Armstrong ... and him. That was it now. Another guerrilla hove into view alongside, lips curled into a grin as he aimed a bullet at the rancher. Prince fired at point-blank range. The raider threw up his arms, slid from his running horse.

Armstrong triggered his weapon with cool regularity, pausing only to reload. Prince guessed he'd figured him wrong ... Mrs. Russell, too. She was a huddled, silent shape between the cattleman and Kirby. He glanced to the girl. Her face had paled, but, when she saw him looking, she smiled faintly.

Shots from the guerrillas had slackened. They were behind the coach now, on the road, regrouping. Colegrove's unexpected decision to barrel straight through them had caught them unawares, thrown them off balance. But it would be for only a few moments; already they were beginning to give chase.

Prince made a hasty calculation. Still a dozen or more in the raiding party. He and Armstrong could not hope to hold them off for long. He thrust his head through the window, looked beyond the wildly running team. A distance to the right he saw a low structure standing beside the road.

"That place ... ?" he yelled at Colegrove. "What is it?"

"Baker's Ranch. Deserted. Not much."

"Pull in!" the lawman shouted above the hammering of the horses. "Fort up ... our only chance!"

Colegrove bobbed his head in agreement. The team was running free on the downgrade, and brake blocks now began to whine, go silent, whine again as the old driver alternately applied and released them to control the swaying vehicle.

Back on the seat Prince faced the others. "We're pulling off, going to hole up in an old ranch house. Be ready to jump and run for it when I give the word."

He waited for reaction—some pointless protest from Mrs. Russell, a complaint from Armstrong, a note of despair from the girl. None came. Dave Kirby lifted his chained wrists.

"Take these off, Marshal ... and give me my gun. I'll help."

Prince grunted. "Forget it. All you need do is run for the door of that house when I tell you."

He threw his glance back down the road. In the dust-filled distance he could see the dim outlines of the raiders pounding in pursuit. They were nearer than he expected. Abruptly the coach was rocking dangerously, and the brakes were a constant screaming as they wheeled from the main ruts. The vehicle skidded, tipped on two wheels, and for a breathless instant John Prince thought they would overturn, but the coach righted itself and plunged on.

"Get ready!"

Prince shouted his warning above the crackling of the wood, protesting the savage treatment. He looked through the window. The ranch house was just ahead. He turned then to the road. The guerrillas were curving in toward them, beginning to shoot again. Colegrove yelled something, and the coach began to slide, skidding close to the building.

"Now!" Prince cried and, flinging the door open, leaped out. He dropped to one knee, began to fire at the oncoming horsemen, conscious of the other passengers streaming by him. Above, on the box, Colegrove had taken up Drummond's rifle, was giving him aid. He looked over his shoulder. The two women and Armstrong were already inside the adobe-walled hut. Kirby was standing in the doorway.

At once the lawman began to back toward the structure, shooting steadily with both pistols at the raiders. "Colegrove!" he yelled. "Come on ... inside!"

Lead slugs were thudding into the thick wall behind him, into the wood of the coach, kicking up dust around his feet.

"Colegrove!" he shouted again.

He gained the doorway, saw then that Colegrove could not hear. The driver lay half off the coach seat, head hanging, a broad circle of red staining his shirt front. Prince took a long step. He felt the solid smash of a bullet as it drove into his thigh. It spun him around. Instantly he felt Kirby's hands grab him into the shadowy interior of the house. Angered, he shook off the outlaw, booted the door shut, and dropped the bar into place. In that identical instant he heard the pound of hoofs and a surge of yells as the riders thundered into the yard. It had been close.

He wheeled, ignoring pain, knowing exactly what must be done—the other door barricaded, the wooden shutters closed and secured. Surprise ran through him when he saw that Armstrong and the women had already performed those vital chores, and there was for John Prince a brief moment of wonder at his bitter judgment of his fellow passengers.

"You've been hit!" Mrs. Russell exclaimed, hurrying toward him.

"Nothing serious," the lawman snapped, and moved to one of the front windows. He peered through a crack. "They'll be rushing us, but it won't be long till dark. If we can hold them off that long, like as not they'll give up and wait for morning."

Armstrong said—"Right."—in a business-like way. "I'll take the other door."

The house, a squat, one-room affair, evidently had been built for just such a critical moment except the owner would have had Indian attacks in mind. At each of the two doors and windows were small, round ports, blocked now by rags filled with sand. Prince pulled the bags away, looked again into the yard. The guerrillas had withdrawn fifty yards or so. They were in the process of bringing up a log they'd obtained from one of the decaying corrals.

"Armstrong," Prince called without turning. "They're aiming to ram the door, break it in. Get up here and cover this other port."

The cattleman crossed the room quickly, stationed himself at the small opening.

There was a sudden flurry of covering gunshots, the sound of bullets driving into the adobe bricks. A chorus of wild yells lifted, and then a half a dozen men supporting the log between them rushed for the door.

Cool, Prince said: "Take the lead man on the right. I'll handle the left. Don't miss.

He waited until the guerrillas were not more than ten paces away, fired. His target was a squat, dark-faced man wearing an ill-assorted uniform of both armies. The raider halted abruptly, fell. A step behind him the one singled out by Armstrong, hands clawing at his chest, was sinking to the ground. The remaining men, stalled by surprise, dropped the log and fled, evidently having overlooked the ports. Prince felled a third as they turned tail.

He was aware then of Mrs. Russell kneeling at his side. She had a strip of white cloth, probably ripped from her petticoat, draped across her shoulder and a knife in her hand. Deftly she slit the leg of his trousers.

"Never mind," he said, and tried to move away.

"Stand still," she replied sternly. "You're losing too much blood."

He looked down at her. Kate was like that. A little bossy when need be—and it mattered to her. Armstrong's voice caught his attention.

"Stopped 'em cold. Fact is, couple of

them are pulling out."

Prince glanced through his port. "Going for the rest of their bunch, I suspect. Seems we're going to be encircled. Means they aim to pin us down for the night."

"Be dark soon," Armstrong commented.

Mrs. Russell, her job completed, stepped back. Prince shifted his weight to the injured member. It was paining considerably now, and getting stiff. It would be giving him hell later.

The acrid smoke was clearing from the room. Martha Russell turned to the cattleman. "When the stage doesn't arrive at the next station, will they send somebody to find out why?"

"Hard to say," the cattleman answered. "Only one stop between here and Silver City, and that's a team change. This run's a bit irregular. Not apt to start thinking about it until noon, maybe even later."

Prince was fingering the ammunition in the bandanna. He glanced to Armstrong. "How many bullets you got?"

There was a moment of silence. Then: "Four rounds. You?"

"Dozen or so. Don't think we can depend on that bunch out there not making another try before morning. Best we stand watch at all four sides." He pivoted awkwardly, forgetting momentarily his injured leg, addressed Mrs. Russell. "You shoot a pistol?"

"A little ... I'm not sure."

From the depths of their murky quarters Dave Kirby spoke up. "Better give me that gun, Marshal."

"We'll get along without your help," the lawman answered.

"I don't know about that," Armstrong broke in doubtfully. "Ought to have a man, good with a gun, helping ..."

"No prisoner of mine gets his hands on a weapon," Prince stated flatly. "I'll accept no help from one, either."

Mrs. Russell sighed audibly. "You're a foolish man. And one who's never learned the meaning of trust ... or faith."

"You're figuring him right, ma'am," Kirby said, a thread of amusement in his voice. "He don't believe in nobody but himself ... not even his own wife."

John Prince stiffened in the darkness.

"That way a man never gets hurt," he said. "How about taking your stations?" He handed Kirby's gun to Mrs. Russell.

The minutes wore on, dragged into an hour, and night's chill settled over the room. Outside a half dozen small fires marked the positions of the raiders ringing the structure. Prince thought of Kate, wondered what she was doing at that moment. Immediately that sharp uneasiness began to gnaw at him. Was she with Wilson Coyle? Maybe with some other man he wasn't even aware of? And then another thought reached him. Perhaps it would all end here. Perhaps the raiders would settle the whole problem for him—for her.

"Got any ideas what you'll be doing come the morning?" Dave Kirby asked, breaking the hush. "You got maybe fifteen bullets, Marshal. How long do you figure you can stand off that bunch?"

"Long enough."

"For what? They hit us from all four sides at once, and the ball will be over ... for sure if they've got help coming."

Armstrong's voice showed interest. "You got something in mind?"

Kirby said: "Was I to get out of here and find me a horse, I could leg it for the next station, stir up a posse ... maybe soldiers, even. They'd be here by sunrise."

"Could at that," Armstrong said. "Where'd you get a horse? Them raiders won't ..."

"Take one of the coach team. Still standing out there in front. What do you say, Marshal? Don't care nothing about myself, or you either, for that matter, but I sure hate to think of what'll happen to these ladies."

Prince sagged against the wall, taking the weight off his injured leg. "You'd try anything to keep from facing that judge in Rinconada," he said in a dry, sarcastic voice. "Well, you're not fooling me. Once you went through that door, you'd line out straight for Mexico."

"Figured you'd be thinking that," the outlaw said. "Only you're plumb wrong. I can make it past them ridge-runners out there. You got my word I'll be waiting at the station for you."

Prince shorted. "Your word? Forget it, mister. I wouldn't trust you ..." He stopped, feeling the hard circle of a gun's muzzle pressing into his ribs.

"I'm sorry," Mrs. Russell's voice, calm and confident, reached him. "I believe him. Make no mistake," she added quickly and prodded harder with the weapon as the lawman stirred. "I know enough about this weapon to pull the trigger ... and this close I couldn't miss. At this moment I'm a desperate woman ... a mother, and I'll do anything to keep my daughter from falling into the hands of those ... those beasts out there. If Mister Kirby is willing to risk his life for us, I say we let him do so."

"You're a fool," Prince said in deep disgust. "He won't go for help. He's not interested in anything except a chance to get where the law can't touch him."

"I don't think so," the woman replied firmly. "Maybe it's your profession that's turned you hard ... hard and bitter ... and made you forget that there's usually some good in the worst of us."

"Usually, but not in this case," Prince said dryly. "Armstrong?"

"I agree with the lady," the cattleman said. "Our only chance."

"You saying you believe he'll do what he claims?"

"I'm willing to gamble on it. Comes a time, Marshal, when you've got to trust somebody. Man can't go forever depending on himself. It's a question of having faith."

"Faith!" John Prince echoed scornfully, his thoughts, oddly, swinging to Kate. There was no value in faith, no substance—just as there was none in trust. Believe in either and a man found only heartbreak and disillusionment. Had he not learned that the hard way? Perhaps he had no real proof concerning Kate, but the signs were all there—at least, what he considered indications. And true, she had denied them all, reproved him for his suspicions. But a man was a fool to ignore common logic.

"Just you stand easy," Armstrong's voice bored into his consciousness. "I'll be getting the keys for them handcuffs."

John Prince offered no resistance. He stood aside, watched them release Kirby, saw Mrs. Russell pass Kirby's gun to him, heard Armstrong murmur—"Good luck, boy."—and then his prisoner was slipping through the door opened only slightly. A heavy sigh escaped Prince. This was it. The end. He'd lost all ... all.

★ ★ ★ ★ ★

The long night finally was over. The first flare of light began to spread across the plains, and the shadows took on form. The two women, pale and worn from their vigilance, turned from the window ports. Armstrong forsook the rear door, noting that the encirclement had been withdrawn from around the shack. He stooped, peered through one of the front openings.

"About twice as many of them out there now," he said wearily. "Seems they've rousted out the head man."

Leg paining him intensely, Prince turned, glanced through his port. A lean individual in a gray Confederate Army uniform was in the center of the guerrilla party. He appeared to be outlining a plan to his followers.

"Looks like the boy got away," Armstrong commented. "Lead team horse is gone, and there ain't no bodies except them three we cut down yesterday laying out there."

"He made it," Prince said. "Has that kind of luck. Right now I'd say he was halfway to the border." He paused, squinted into the glare. "Get yourself set. They're going to hit us. Don't waste no lead. We've only got ..."

His words broke off. Faintly, riding the cold, clear air of the early morning, the notes of a bugle carried to him. Prince, disbelief covering his face, turned to Armstrong, then to Mrs. Russell—to the girl. The thrilling sound grew louder, closer. Abruptly guns began to crackle.

There was a quick rush of pounding hoofs, and through the port Prince saw a line of blue-clad riders, some with sabers flashing, sweep into the yard. More gunfire crashed. Two of the cavalrymen spilled from their horses; a half dozen guerrillas went down; others raced for their mounts. The line of blue swerved, gave chase.

"He did it!" Armstrong yelled happily, struggling with the bar that locked the door. "By heaven, the boy did it!"

John Prince shook his head. "Doubt that. Expect those soldiers were just riding by ... happened to spot ..."

But the others were hurrying through the open door, smiling, laughing, grateful for their rescue, for the warming sun. The cavalry came into view again, a portion of it swinging on westward, a smaller detail cutting away, slanting toward the stranded stagecoach and its passengers. A waxed-mustached major with a round, sun-

them all ... every last one of them."

Mrs. Russell, once again a woman, began to weep softly, sought comfort in her daughter's arms.

Armstrong took a deep breath. "Was close," he said. "That young cowboy ... did he get through all right? Without getting hurt, I mean."

The officer smiled again. "Well, from here to where we're bivouacked it's around twenty miles. He rode the whole distance bareback and at a fast clip. He'll find standing most comfortable for a few days. Otherwise, he's fine. And by the way, Marshal," he added, swiveling his attention to Prince, "said he was your prisoner. Soon

burned face came in ahead of his men, slowed, his eyes on the coach team.

"Corporal Hayes!" he barked. "Catch up one of those stray mounts and hitch him into harness so these people can continue on their journey."

The officer moved in nearer to the house, halted. He saluted gravely, said: "Major Amos Allingham, at your service. We'll have you ready to move out in a few minutes. Pleased to see none of you has been seriously injured."

Allingham hesitated, looked over his shoulder where three of his yellowlegs were getting the coach ready. A smile pulled at his lips. "Want to thank you for dispatching that young cowboy to us. We've been hunting those guerrillas for weeks. Got

as he gave me the information I needed, he put himself in my custody. You'll find him waiting in my tent."

John Prince stared at the officer. Somewhere, deep within his mind, a door opened, a wide door beyond which a pure white light shown brilliantly. He'd been wrong about Dave Kirby. There were others he'd been wrong about, too, most likely. And Kate ... maybe he was wrong there. It was possible ... no, probable. He could see that now. He'd been a fool, a great fool ... and all that Mrs. Russell and Armstrong, the cattleman, had said he was.

He turned to them. There was a smile on his lips, the first they'd seen since he had boarded the stage. "I'm glad Kirby got through. Took a lot of sand, and, when he goes before the judge in Rinconada, like for you to be there with us. Maybe if we all speak up, tell what he did, we can help things along for him a bit."

"Count on me," Armstrong said fervently.

Mrs. Russell bobbed her head. "I'll speak to my husband. Perhaps he can do something."

Prince swung back to Allingham. "Our thanks to you, too, Major, for getting here when you did."

"My job, sir," the officer said, and start-

ed to pull away.

"One more thing," John Prince called after him. "You have a telegraph wire connection at your camp?"

Allingham nodded. "Hooked in temporarily with the main line."

"Good. Like to send my wife a message, tell her I'll be home shortly."

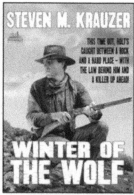

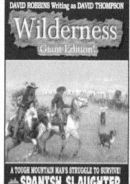

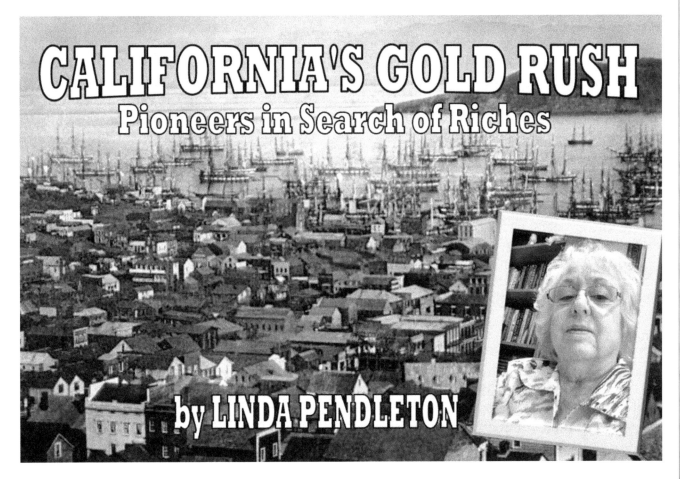

CALIFORNIA'S GOLD RUSH
Pioneers in Search of Riches
by LINDA PENDLETON

"Dreams are the touchstones of our character. "
~Henry David Thoreau (1817-1862)

In January, 1848, an event occurred in the Northern California foothills of the Sierra Nevada Mountains that would significantly change the future of the territory.

James W. Marshall discovered gold while constructing a sawmill for John Sutter along the American River in Coloma, California. The discovery received little notice, partly because many did not believe it, but that changed by late 1848 as word began to spread.

Then ... the Gold Rush was on!

Gold seekers came from all over America, overland, or by sea, to San Francisco. Prior to the Gold Rush, the population of San Francisco was less than 500 people. By the end of 1849, the population of the city was approximately 25,000, and the surrounding area had grown to an estimated 100,000. The 1852 state population was more than 250,000, and many of those people were in Northern California, and numbers were more than 350,000 two years later.

The excitement was not confined to the United States. France held lotteries and the holders of winning tickets were given a trip to the California gold fields. The French found their way to California, many from Canada, others from their homeland. In Great Britain, Ireland, Norway, to a certain extent in Germany, South America, China, Mexico, and even Australia, the adventurous and impoverished were pricking up their ears and laying their plans to head to California and find their gold treasure.

Some came to take advantage of the need for services and businesses, not only in the Sierra foothill mining areas, but in San Francisco, Sacramento, Stockton, and other growing cities. Commerce would play an important part as towns were set up or growing with the influx of people. As communities sprung into being, so did related problems—government, or lack of—politics, fair or dirty—corruption and crime—social chaos and disorder—education and transportation—cultural diversity and prejudice—and many other challenges.

Thomas Farish was fifteen years of age when he came to California in 1852 with his mother and siblings aboard ship. His father had traveled across land from Tennessee nearly three years earlier to prospect for gold, and after having established himself in Northern California in the town of Marysville as a pie store merchant, and after the Panama Canal opened making travel easier, he arranged for his family to join him in the Golden State.

These were the words Farish wrote later about seeing California for the first time: "In April, 1852, the 'Northerner' passed safely through the famous Golden Gate. As she glided proudly into the majestic bay, the beautiful peninsula of San Francisco lying to the right, pretty islands dotting the waters around, and stretching to the left, the inviting lands of Contra Costa—where now lies the city of Oakland—all, heightened by the blue sky and glorious sunshine of California, were enough to inspire the heart and arouse the enthusiasm of the most sluggish natures known."

Young Thomas Farish became employed by a San Francisco trading firm, and then in 1856 began gold mining on the Feather River.

In the pristine areas of the Feather River lived Native Americans known as the *Maidu*. They resided in the central Sierra Nevada Mountain Range, in the Sierra Valley, in the drainage area of the Feather and American Rivers, and in the Sacramento Valley. They were hunters and gatherers, and were exemplary basket makers, weaving highly detailed, intricate, and useful baskets of all sizes. In the late 1700s, it was estimated their population was around 9,000, but by a 1930 census they numbered only 31. Today their population is approximately 3,500.

Today the Feather River waters are an important part of the water source for California.

Having been born myself in California, I know well the beauty of the state, and how it offers a variety of terrain, from the coastal waters of the Pacific Ocean and the coastal mountains, to the inland Sierra Nevada mountain range rising up to 14,505 feet of Mt. Whitney, the highest summit in the contiguous United States, and to the more arid desert lands of the Mojave and the contrast of the lowest point of Death Valley at 282 feet below sea level. We have mountains capped with winter's snow, crystal clear lakes, rushing mountain streams and rivers, the lush forests with ferns, tall pines and Redwoods, the Oak covered foothills, colorful rose gardens and vegetable gardens, green grass and desert cacti, fruit trees and grape vines, coastal cliffs and sandy beaches, and even with all that within the borders of California, we also have a history rich in drama.

In 1867-1869, Thomas Edwin Farish was a member of the California State Assembly, 8th District, and in his later years, he left California and made his home in Tombstone, Arizona, and later, Phoenix. From June of 1912 until his death in Octo-

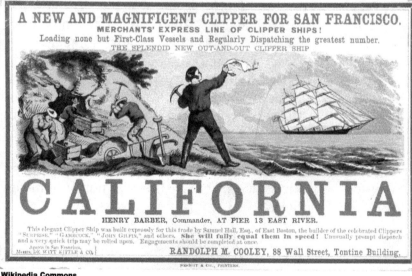

28

ber of 1919, he was the Arizona State Historian. Shortly after his death, his eighth volume of the *History of Arizona* was published, the first volume published in 1915.

Farish was also involved as a mine inspector and mine boss with the Vulture Mine near Wickenburg, Arizona, not far from Phoenix, and in 1894 his lease expired on the mine. The Vulture Mine was discovered by Henry Wickenburg in 1863, and closed for good in 1942 after 200 million dollars worth of gold was taken from the mine. From 1863 to 1942, the mine produced 340,000 ounces of gold and 260,000 ounces of silver, and has been credited with founding the town of Wickenburg.

Back in California over a ten-year period from the first discovery of gold in 1848, launching the '49 Gold Rush, more than 775 million was found in gold in California mines. By the end of the nineteenth century it is said several billion dollars worth of gold came out of California mines.

According to the California State Parks Department, the non-Indian population of California in 1848 when James Marshall discovered gold at Sutter's Mill in Coloma, was 14,000. By the end of 1849, it had risen

Wikipedia Commons

to nearly 100,000, and by 1852 it was some 250,000. The gold fever brought many looking for riches and opportunity. And many found it, not always in prospecting, but through commerce for the bulging and needy population.

As San Francisco flourished as a great port of entry for the Pacific Coast, facilities for shipping rapidly multiplied in the bay area and before long, inland to Sacramento.

In 1869, one of the largest gold nuggets ever discovered in California was found at the Monumental Mine near Sierra Buttes north of Sacramento, and it weighed in at 106 pounds. Eleven mines and arrastras were situated in and around the Buttes.

California became a state of the Union in 1850, being the 31st state and entered the Union as a free, non-slavery state by the Compromise of 1850. San Jose was the first Capital, but after a harsh wet winter of '50-'51 and because it did not have proper facilities, the final choice in 1854, was to move the Capital inland on the Sacramento Delta to the riverside port of Sacramento, where it is today.

Sacramento was where John Sutter had a farm and a fort. Sutter's Fort had played a role in the Bear Flag Revolt of 1846, when control of California was the point of dissension. John Sutter Jr., in the absence of his father, founded the town of Sacramento, a short distance from Sutter's Fort. The Fort is now a National Historic Landmark.

From the time California set out to become a state in 1849, the Greek word, *Eureka,* which means "I have found it," was the state motto.

Of course, it is assumed that *Eureka* refers to the discovery of gold.

While a member of the California State Legislator, Democrat Thomas Edwin Farish introduced the San Francisco Tide Lands Bill which saved the tidelands area of the city by the Golden Gate. Farish was also a friend and follower of Henry George. George, a Lincoln Republican who then became a Democrat, was an author and political activist. He was a strong critic of mining and railroad interests, corrupt politicians, labor contractors, and land speculators. In 1879, George published his successful book, *Progress and Poverty*, which sold over 3 million copies.

The Chinese immigrants were very much a part of the Gold Rush days and the building of the railroads, and even in positions of government service. Both men, Farish and George, held the belief that Chinese immigration should be restricted, and Farish was outspoken about that.

James Martin Peebles, (*Seers of the Ages*, 1869) wrote of meeting a Chinese man while he was in California during that time. "In 1861, at Placerville, introduced to Le Can, a learned Mandarin, who graduated from a Chinese University, and was then employed as interpreter in the courts of California. Highly intelligent, he was proud of his national literature."

Peebles returned to California in 1872 and this is some of what he wrote in his 1875 book, *Around the World Travels*: "Landing upon the Pacific coast, I can only now exclaim, What changes! What a marvelous growth! The State has a population of some six hundred thousand; the city of San Francisco, one hundred and fifty thousand. Citizenship here is a conglomerate. Pioneer Californians are truly hospitable. El-Dorado men are proverbially generous. Those possessing fortunes are certainly more liberal with them than the same number in the bleaker Atlantic cities. Money should be yoked to education, and idealism harnessed to practical uses. Financially Californian cups run over. This is the trouble,—the material overriding the spiritual. The two themes of excitement just now are continental railways and Arizona diamond-fields. Reality or sham diamond stocks sell readily; and emigrants, vying with miners are hurrying along the trails of the troublesome Apaches."

Farish wrote what it meant to be a Californian, a pioneer, a prospector, who came to America, the land of plenty, and to the Golden State of California, across land, and by sea, with hopes and dreams to find his or her fortune. As he stated: "But often those who in quest of gold explore new lands, build better than they dream of. So it was with those who in the days of old, in days of gold, in the days of 'Forty-nine,' were the pioneers of California. Their enterprise, their intelligence and their industry laid broad and deep the foundations of the empire of the Pacific Slope. Not California alone, but Nevada, Idaho and Arizona as well. They promoted the imperial city of San Francisco, where the argosies of the world, passing her Golden Gate, stop to pay tribute to her commercial supremacy. And best of all, bequeathed to those who came after them civic virtues so great that to be a Californian, in the truest sense is to be a broad-minded, liberal, brave and generous man. One whose word is his bond, whose honesty is unquestioned, and whose patriotism is intensely sublime. The entire Pacific Coast felt the new impetus given by mining. The prospectors with their burros started on their tours of discovery more elated and hopeful than ever, and many new mining districts were opened up. Not only in Nevada, but in Utah, Idaho, Montana, Arizona and Old Mexico."

Another pioneer who joined the journey westward in the spring of 1849, did so on his doctor's orders. He was told to "go West" for a change of climate and that more exertion would be good for him following an illness of "consumption."

That man was Alonzo Delano, born July 2, 1806, in Aurora, New York, the tenth child of Dr. Frederick Delano, a physician and his wife, Joann Dotty Delano.

Alonzo Delano left school at a young age and not long after became a merchant. In 1830, he married Mary Burt, and relocated his family to Ottawa, Illinois by 1848. He sold bank stocks, food, and wares, and became a well-respected community leader.

After deciding to take his doctor's suggestion, even though he was sick and often suffering from fevers, he shipped his belongings and cattle to join the Dayton Company of travelers at St. Joseph, Missouri, leaving his wife and two children behind in Illinois.

He had made arrangements with several newspapers to record his journey across the plains to California and the gold mines. As a writer, his prose was humorous, factual, and entertaining. It was said his humor was similar to Mark Twain's, and was one of the first writers to use what become known as "California Humor," a style of writing that uses sa-

tirical social commentary, exaggerated situations, and whimsical sketches of miners, gamblers, Indians, and other pioneers.

During most of the perilous journey, Delano was ill with fever. The journey was on the Oregon Trail from St. Joseph, Missouri, along the Platte River, through the South Pass west of Laramie, Wyoming, and southwest on the California Trail along the Humboldt River through Idaho, Nevada and into Northern California. But somehow he found the strength to continue the journey with all the obstacles and hardships the wagon trains faced: lack of food, water, injuries, hostile Indians, bad weather, flooding, dying cattle, and other problems.

Delano arrived in California in September, 1849. He went to work mining in the Marysville, Yuba River area for a short time. He soon after established a produce business in San Francisco. Following a waterfront fire, he left San Francisco for the town of Grass Valley, California, and there he began mining.

In 1850, he purchased a claim located not far from Grass Valley. But when it proved not to be very productive he sold his interest in it.

In Grass Valley, he concentrated on be-

Wikipedia Commons

ing a storekeeper. He was elected as the first town treasurer. In 1854, he began working for Wells Fargo and Company in Sacramento and became Grass Valley's first Wells Fargo Agent.

Alonzo Delano, Photo Courtesy of Wikipedia Commons

In an 1856 book, *Old Block's Sketch Book*, Delano wrote of the September 13, 1855, devastating fire that swept through Grass Valley, destroying hundreds of homes, business and possessions. Delano wrote: "On the eventful night which laid our town in ruins, which left us no cover for our heads but the blue vault of Heaven; did you hear one word of wailing?-one single note of despair? No, not one."

One of the items that survived the devastating fire was the Wells Fargo safe. With the town in ruins, Delano wheeled a small shed to the location of the burned out Wells Fargo office and set up a temporary office. He opened the safe, still warm to the touch, but documents and currency were in fine order. He told his depositors to come get their deposits and they would have what was theirs "as long as there is a dollar in the safe." The people needed to have that sense of security and the hope that all good be

good again.

Five days later he opened his own bank and immediately received more deposits than he had previously held.

He wrote about the lack of law and order, at the time California was granted statehood in 1850. "The announcement, then, that California was finally, though grudgingly, admitted as a State, and that the acts of her people were confirmed, was hailed with joy, and bonfires were kindled, artillery pealed, and acclamations resounded in every town throughout the length and breadth of the land, for the people of California loved their brethren at home, and above all, the glorious Union of States which bound them in one common tie; and also ardently desired the 'star spangled banner' should wave over her mountains and plains, a symbol that this too was 'the land of the free, the home of the brave.' San Francisco took the lead, and processions, orations, odes and illuminations, and general rejoicings were the order of the day. The thousand ships which proudly floated in its magnificent harbor, were gaily decked with streamers; gun after gun boomed over its placid waters. In a moment all feeling of irritation ceased, and could our Atlantic brethren have witnessed the general joy, they would have gladly joined in the prolonged shout of 'the Union, now and forever!'

"But an evil had taken root, which grew out of the previous existing state of things, and which at one time threatened to overturn all law and order, in fact, government itself. The gold of California had attracted to its shores the dissolute and dishonest from all countries of the civilized globe. Situated within reach of the penal colonies of Great Britain, as well as being in proximity with the semi-barbarous hordes of Spanish America, whose whole history is that of revolution and disorder, it was soon flooded by great numbers from those countries, who were accomplished in crime, and who, without feeling any sympathy for our institutions, and contributing nothing for the support of our government, their only aim seemed to be to obtain gold, by any means, no matter how fraudulent; and owing to the weakness of the constituted authorities, joined to the vicious among our own people, they succeeded in their frauds and crimes to an amazing extent, and rendered the security of life and property a paradox on legislation, hitherto unprecedented in the annals of modern history."

Delano returned to Illinois and moved his family to Grass Valley. He died September 8, 1874, and because he was admired by the town's people, all business in Grass Valley suspended operations to honor him.

Delano's book, *Life on the Plains and Among the Diggings, 1853,* describes the hardships, the tragedies, the triumphs, the social interactions, in a well-crafted examination of life in the Gold Rush days, the founding of new communities, and the development of laws and culture during the formation of the Golden State of California.

J. D. Borthwick, at the age of twenty-three, came to the United States in 1847 from his home in Edinburgh Scotland. In May of 1853, he caught the Gold Rush fever and arrived in California. In 1857, he published an article in *Harper's Weekly* and then in a book, *Three Years in California*, with descriptions of mining techniques, personal interactions, transportation, crime, events, hotels and restaurants, entertainment and the social life of the era and growth of California. It focused on his experiences and encounters in gold camps. He wrote, "The Americans are often accused of boasting—perhaps deservedly so; but there certainly are many things in the history of California of which they may just-

ly be proud, having transformed her, as they did so suddenly, from a wilderness into a country in which most of the luxuries of life were procurable; and a fair instance of the bold and prompt spirit of commercial enterprise by which this was accomplished, was seen in the fact that, from the earliest days of her settlement, California had as good means of both ocean and inland steam-communication as any of the oldest countries in the world."

We've heard a lot about gambling in the Wild West, and as authors we may write

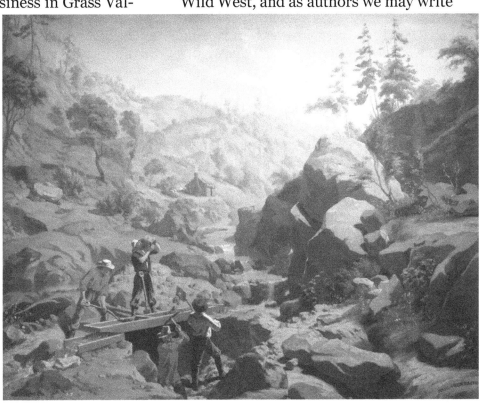

"Miners in the High Sierras", painted by Frederick August Wenderoth, Courtesy of Wikipedia Commons

about gamblers within our novels. Here is a well thought-out descriptive overview of who we might have found at a gambling table during the Gold Rush days, by J.D. Borthwick. "The gambling saloons were very numerous, occupying the most prominent positions in the leading thoroughfares, and all of them presenting a more conspicuous appearance than the generality of houses around them. They were thronged

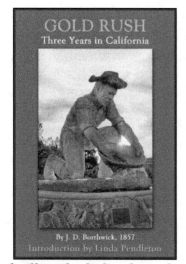

day and night, and in each was a very good band of music, the performers being usually German or French.

"On entering a first-class gambling room, one found a large, well-proportioned saloon sixty or seventy feet long, brilliantly lighted up by several very fine chandeliers, the walls decorated with ornamental painting and gilding, and hung with large mirrors and showy pictures, while in an elevated projecting orchestra half-a-dozen Germans were playing operatic music. There were a dozen or more tables in the room, each with a compact crowd of eager betters around it, and the whole room was so filled with men that elbowing one's way between the tables was a matter of difficulty. The atmosphere was quite hazy with the quantity of tobacco smoke, and was strongly impregnated with the fumes of brandy. If one happened to enter while the musicians were taking a rest, the quiet stillness were remarkable. Nothing was heard but a slight hum of voices, and the constant chinking of money; for it was the fashion, while standing betting at a table, to have a lot of dollars in one's hands, and to keep shuffling them backwards and forwards like so many cards.

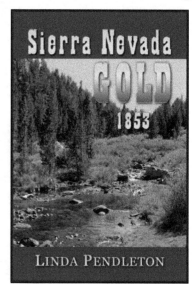

"The people composing the crowd were men of every class, from the highest to the lowest, and though the same as might be seen elsewhere, their extraordinary variety of character and of dress appeared still more curious from their being brought into such close juxtaposition, and apparently placed upon an equality. Seated round the same table might be seen well-dressed respectable-looking men, and, alongside of them, rough miners fresh from the diggings, with well-filled buckskin purses, dirty old flannel shirts, and shapeless hats; jolly tars half-seas over, not understanding anything about the game, nor apparently taking any interest in it, but having their spree out at the gaming-table because it was the fashion, and good-humouredly losing their pile of five or six hundred or a thousand dollars; Mexicans wrapped up in their blankets smoking *cigaritas*, and watching the game intently from under their broad-brimmed hats; Frenchmen in their blouses smoking black pipes; and little urchins, or little old scamps rather, ten or twelve years of age, smoking cigars as big as themselves, with the air of men who were quite up to all the hooks and crooks of this wicked world (as indeed they were), and losing their hundred dollars at a pop with all the nonchalance of an old gambler; while crowds of men, some dressed like gentlemen, and mixed with all sorts of nondescript ragamuffins, crowded round, and stretched over those seated at the tables, in order to make their bets.

"There were dirty, squalid, villainous-looking scoundrels, who never looked straight out of their eyes, but still were always looking at something, as if they were 'making a note of it,' and who could have made their faces their fortunes in some parts of the world, by 'sitting' for murderers, or ruffians generally.

"Occasionally one saw, jostled about unresistingly by the crowd, and as if the crowd ignored its existence, the live carcass of some wretched, dazed, woebegone man, clad in the worn-out greasy habiliments of quondam gentility; the glassy unintelligent eye looking as if no focus could be found for it, but as if it saw a dim misty vision of everything all at once; the only meaning in the face being about the lips, where still lingered the smack of grateful enjoyment of the last mouthful of whisky, blended with a longing humble sigh for the speedy recurrence of any opportunity of again experiencing such an awakening bliss, and forcibly expressing an unquenchable thirst for strong drinks, together with the total absence of all power to do anything towards relieving it, while the whole appearance of the man spoke of bitter disappointment and reverses, without the force to bear up under them. He was the picture of sottish despair, and the name of his duplicates was legion.

"There was in the crowd a large proportion of sleek well-shaven men, in stovepipe hats and broadcloth; but, however nearly a man might approach in appearance to the conventional idea of a gentleman, it is not to be supposed, on that account, that he either was, or got the credit of being, a bit better than his neighbors. The man standing next to him, in the guise of a laboring man, was perhaps his superior in wealth, character, and education. Appearances, at least as far as dress was concerned, went for nothing at all. A man was judged by the amount of money in his purse, and frequently the man to be most courted for his dollars was the most to be despised for his looks.

"One element of mixed crowds of people, in the States and in this country, was very poorly represented. There were scarcely any of the lower order of Irish; the cost of emigration to California was at that time too great for the majority of that class, although now the Irish population of San Francisco is nearly equal in proportion to that in the large cities of the Union."

Don't you agree that Borthwick gives us colorful visuals of the diversity of customers in the California Gold Rush gambling saloons?

In reading the history of my home state, I've learned interesting facts about those people, the culture of the time, the hardships they faced, their successes, their failures, the humor, their talents, the scoundrels and villains, the grief, and the everyday life during the mid-1800s. And because J. D. Borthwick, James Martin Peebles, Alonzo Delano, and Thomas Farish lived it, they were able to colorfully record how a state came into being with diverse cultures mixing and finding their way in new environments, and reaching for their dreams. Some of those pioneers found their dreams, others enriched theirs, and still others failed, but all were determined, setting risks aside, and often finding courage to go on. They were no different than us.

And gold? Yes, it is still here in California.

In the summer of 2008, a teenager, Jacob Hopkins, who shares a hobby of gold prospecting with his father and older brother, discovered a smooth rock with six ounces of gold while fishing at Rollins Lake in Nevada County near Grass Valley. The local teenager's find was worth $5,500. He spotted its shine near the edge of the water, and is quoted as saying, "I went out there and grabbed it, and I was like 'oh my gosh that can't be gold—it is.'"

Interesting enough, his father, Mike Hopkins, relates to his son's discovery as he had a similar experience twenty-six years before when he was a teenager. "I was going to go slew some gold to go to the senior prom, and about second shovel a four ounce gold nugget rolled right in the tip of my shovel."

Well, who knows?

Maybe there are more gold nuggets yet to be discovered.

Linda Pendleton has written in a variety of genres: nonfiction, novels, comic book scripting, ecourses, screenplays and poetry. She has published three novels in her *Catherine Winter Private Investigator* Series. Other novels include *The Unknown*; *Sound of Silence*; *Deadly Flare-Up;* and the historical novel, *Corn Silk Days, Iowa 1862*. Linda has published several nonfiction books; and has written introductions to various 19th century books on early California history. She coauthored several books with her late husband, author Don Pendleton, including the crime novel, *Roulette: The Search for the Sunrise Killer;* and the nonfiction books, *To Dance With Angels* and *Whispers From the Soul*. She lives in the West and enjoys family genealogy when not writing. She is currently writing a Western novel. Her website is http://lindapendleton.com

PETER MCCURTIN
A PERSONAL APPRECIATION
BY
BEN BRIDGES

It's a curious paradox that one of the most popular, best and proficient exponents of the hard-boiled western novel also happens to be one of its least-known. Indeed, for many years, fans wondered if Peter McCurtin was a real author, or merely a house name behind which a small army of scribes produced some of the toughest and most compelling westerns of the 1970s and 80s. As dedicated researcher Lynn Munroe of www.lynn-munroe-books.com has since discovered, however ... he was actually both!

The real Peter J. McCurtin was born in Ireland on October 15, 1929, and immigrated to America when he was in his early twenties. He worked as associate editor and editor respectively on *All-Man Magazine* and *Cavalcade, and* in 1958, co-edited the short-lived (one issue) *New York Review* with William Atkins. By the early 1960s, he was co-owner of a bookstore in Ogunquit, Maine, and often spent his summers there. Later, he

and his second wife, Mary, shared their home in Ogunquit with a dog that also happened to be part wolf.

McCurtin was working as an editor at Midwood Publishers when he wrote his first novel, *Anything Goes* (1968), the racy story of a pilot juggling five girlfriends at the same time. But his second novel, *Sex Service* (1969), was actually the work of a high school principal

named George Harmon Smith, who would go on to become McCurtin's favorite ghost-writer. (Other writers to assume the McCurtin alias over the years, working from plots or other material McCurtin supplied, included Aaron Fletcher, Russell Smith, Paul Hofrichter and John Stevenson).

Following a stint at the *National Enquirer,* McCurtin published his breakout book, *Mafioso* (1970). It was nominated for the prestigious Mystery Writers of America Edgar Award, and filmed in 1973 as *The Boss,* with fan favorite Henry Silva. More books in the same vein followed, including *Cosa Nostra* (1971), *Omerta* (1972), *The Syndicate* (1972) and *Escape From Devil's Island* (1972).

1970 also saw the publication of his first *Carmody* western, *Hangtown.*

On the surface, at least, Carmody is just another trail-wise adventurer. Sometimes he

is presented as an outlaw, sometimes as a gun-for-hire. Whatever his current occupation, however, Carmody's eye is always on the main chance, as McCurtin's tough, spare narrative frequently makes plain.

Carmody's exploits set the tone for most of the westerns McCurtin was to write over the next two decades. His view of the frontier is harsh and unforgiving, a place where a man with any sense looks to his own safety, and to hell with everyone else. McCurtin's westerns are fast, violent and chauvinistic, but the violence and sex are seldom overtly explicit. McCurtin further distances his protagonist from other stock western anti-heroes by recounting the series in the kind of hard-boiled first-person style normally associated with the private-eye genre ... of which he was also a master.

In the first book, Carmody is employed by a wealthy mine owner whose daughter

has been abducted and held to ransom. For *The Slavers* (1970) Carmody locks horns with a powerful rancher who treats his Indian employees (who once saved Carmody's life) like slaves. In *Tough Bullet* (1970) Carmody is living high in New Orleans when his money is stolen and he is framed for murder, while in *Screaming on the Wire* (1972) (possibly the best book of the sequence) he tangles with a psychotic killer claiming to be the younger brother of Billy the Kid. In *The Killers* (1972) Carmody pins on a marshal's badge in order to dodge a posse, and finds himself caught between a bunch of outlaws and a clan of hillbilly killers, while one of the weaker novels, *Tall Man Riding* (1973) sees Carmody tracking down the men who attacked him and stole the proceeds of a bank robbery he has just committed.

McCurtin's editor at Leisure Books remembers that he was "a terrific, fluent, natu-

ral writer of action, and a solid researcher for his westerns and mysteries. Leisure did not, in my time [1979-1981], let anyone else write under Peter's name, but Peter wrote under other names in addition to his own by-line. He was a real workhorse with, unfortunately, an alcohol problem (like so many), and without question the very best writer that Leisure was publishing at the time. Perhaps he could have been better and more prolific under better circumstances."

For a while, McCurtin himself also worked as an editor at Leisure Books.

Piccadilly Publishing's very own Len Levinson, author of *The Sergeant, The Searcher* and countless other way-above-average ac-

tion-adventure and western books, built a complete novel (*The Camp,* as by Jonathan Trask) from just thirty pages supplied by McCurtin.

In Justin Marriott's always-excellent *Paperback Fanatic,* Len recalled, "Peter was fifty-something, charming, gentle, jovial, dressed like a college professor, resembled Winston Churchill ... Peter demonstrated how to write violent melodrama populated by believable characters in vivid locales, but didn't layer description because pulp fiction has got to move. His style reminded me of the great Mickey Spillane.

"I was very fond of Peter's warm, affable personality, especially his sardonic sense of humor".

He returned to the western in 1979 to take over the *Sundance* series originally created and written by the late, great Ben Haas, under the pseudonym "John Benteen". In McCurtin's hands, however, Sundance—a half-breed Cheyenne who undertakes various missions to raise funds to fight the corrupt Indian Ring—became a colder, more impersonal figure, more violent and in my opinion far less credible.

Having said that, it should be added that, overall, McCurtin did a reasonable job of continuing Sundance's exploits, producing some interesting action-orientated westerns, among them *Day of the Halfbreeds* (1979) in which Sundance is sent to Canada to infiltrate Louis Riel's Metis movement and eventually stop a rebellion (a plot that is very similar to his Lassiter story, *Gunfight at Ringo Junction*). *Iron Men* (1981), meanwhile, sees Sundance helping the Central Colorado Railroad against the underhand tactics of a much larger competitor. It is also worth mentioning that the 1980 Sundance yarn *Los Olvidados* is a reworking of the earlier Carmody book *The Slavers*.

Midway through his tenure on the Sundance books, McCurtin wrote the adult western series *Jim Saddler*, under the name Gene Curry. This series returned him to the gritty first-person style of narration that made the Carmody books so distinctive. Of the seven books that comprise Saddler's adventures, however, four are little more than straight rewrites of Carmody novels; *A Dirty Way to Die (Tough Bullet)*, *Wildcat Woman (Screaming on the Wire,*

with Jessie James' daughter replacing Billy the Kid's brother), *Colorado Crossing (Hangtown)* and *Hot as a Pistol (The Killers)*. Of the rest, *Yukon Ride* is particularly notable, in that Saddler has to transport the body of a dead judge from the Yukon border to San Franscisco, with surprising results.

Among his final writing projects, he returned to his earlier *Soldier of Fortune* series, which recounts the exploits of a tough mercenary Jim Rainey. These books are also told in the first-person and have a strong ring of authenticity to them. One of them at least, however, was not the work of Peter McCurtin. *Operation Hong Kong*, a cracker of a story, was actually written by Ralph Hayes.

"He churned out a lot of those short westerns and crime stories," remembers another acquaintance. "I also know that he used the pen-name 'Clarence Farmer' once. He took *Soul on Ice* by Eldridge Cleaver and turned it into *Soul on Fire* by Clarence Farmer.

"I almost think it would be safe to say that if you find a book published by Tower or Leisure in the 1970s, that is a blatant knock-off of something else, and the two authors' names are similar (with respect to style or syllables used) that might be one of Peter's.

"When he wrote most of his books, he lived in a studio in Murray Hill, on 39th Street, only a few blocks from the New York offices of Tower Books, which at the time were located at 2 Park Avenue. His building was called the Tuscany Towers back then. It's now a W Hotel. He had a Murphy bed, a kitchenette, and a desk with manual typewriter. There was no phone except for the payphone in the building basement. He liked eating at Automats, he went to the movies several times a week and spent a lot of time reading."

Peter McCurtin died in New York on 27 January 1997. His westerns in particular are distinguished by unusual plots with neatly resolved conclusions, well-drawn secondary characters, regular bursts of action and tight, smooth writing. If you haven't already checked him out, you have quite a treat in store.

NEIL HUNTER

THE KILLING AT TELEGRAPH HILL

Friday – August, 1899

She watched as he fixed the burnished badge to his vest, self-conscious as he stood in front of the mirror. There was no denying the pride she felt as he paused for a moment to stare at his own reflection. It was a special day, this Friday.

It was his first day as Marshal of Telegraph Hill.

Town Marshal Clem Tatum. Her husband. Head of the family.

Arianna Tatum, standing in the hall of their house, folded linen in her arms, gave a gentle cough and Clem turned to look her way.

'Clem Tatum. Marshal of Telegraph Hill,' she said. 'It has a nice ring to it.'

'Let's not make too much of it, Ari,' he said. That was his familiar name for her – Ari. 'It's only a job.'

Self-effacing as usual. Not a grandiose notion in his head. Clem tended to under estimate his worth.

Arianna offered a gentle smile. 'That you won over the other candidates. By what I believe they term as a landslide. No one else came within a country mile. My, they were all so glum when the votes were counted. Especially Sam Brinker. I declare he was ready to curl up a corner and cry like a baby.'

'It's not nice to feel so smug, Ari.'

'Oh, don't play superior to me, Clem Tatum. I was watching when you pinned on that badge just now. I saw that gleam in your eye.'

He turned away from the mirror. In his mid-thirties. Average height, with a nice spread to his shoulders and a shade off being slim. His thick dark hair brushed the collar of his white cotton shirt. The squarish face, strong jaw and blue eyes, all went to make him look younger than his years. The full mustache he wore was an attempt to add gravitas to his appearance, but it did little to conceal the pleasant aspect of his features.

Today he wore a dark suit, pants pulled over polished high boots and a black string tie. The thin-striped vest where he had pinned his badge of office, completed his ensemble – save for the curl brimmed Stetson in his hands now.

'*Gleam*? That was just the light coming off the mirror.'

'Of course, Marshal,' she said.

'Mrs. Tatum, I do believe you are making fun of me.'

'Is that an arrestable offence, Marshal?'

'I'll have to check the rulebook for that.'

Her gentle laughter, as always, pleased him.

Movement in the periphery of his vision made him turn. His nine year old son, Nathanial was standing in the doorway, big eyed as he stared at the badge on his father's vest. The boy was a smaller version of Clem, even down to the expression in his eyes. The thick fall of dark hair. Right now he had a solemn expression on his face and Clem knew exactly what the boy was thinking.

'Being a peace officer doesn't mean I have to carry a gun all the time,' Clem said, smiling.

'But, pa...'

'Your father is right,' Ari said. 'Guns belong in the marshal's office. Not in our home.'

The boy considered for a moment before letting go a deep sigh.

'I suppose. But you will have one when you walk around town.'

'Let's see how things turn out,' Clem said. He reached out to ruffle the boy's hair. 'I don't want to make folks think they've voted in a would-be gunslinger now.'

When he spoke the words a distant, private memory stirred in him. He allowed it to linger a moment.

'Time to go – *Marshal*,' Ari said.

She was three years younger than Clem, a woman who still showed the beauty that had attracted him from the first moment he had set eyes on her. As tall as he was, slimmer, her chestnut hair reaching her shoulders to frame a lively, full-of-life face he never tired of seeing. The hazel eyes sparkled with the joy she showed every waking moment. She leaned forward and brushed her soft lips against his cheek.

'I will see you later,' she said. 'After I've delivered our son to school.'

'Do I have to go?'

Clem set his hat on his head, glanced at the boy. 'Yes, you have to go. My first day or not, it's still a school day.'

'*But...*'

'Nathanial Tatum, do we want the town to think now that your father is Marshal that you can skip school?' Ari said. 'We have to set an example. *Yes*?'

'Yes'm.'

Clem walked to the door and stepped outside, feeling the already rising heat of the day catch him. He walked down the path to the white gate and went on through. The well-trod path leading to town lay bright and dusty under the sun. Tall cottonwood trees edged the path, stirring lazily in the faint breeze. Clem walked in the center of the path, conscious of being watched as he passed the other houses. He sensed movement and swiveled his eyes as he spotted a suited figure moving to intercept him from the house he was passing.

'Good day, *Marshal* Tatum.'

Henry Danbridge, town banker, member of the council, and Clem's friend. In his early forties, Danbridge was a slightly overweight man who dressed in accordance with his position in the community. He was, by far, Clem's most ardent supporter. He had

campaigned tirelessly to have Clem appointed.

'What happened to *Clem*?'

'Now I wouldn't want to be seen as being overly familiar with our officer of the law,' Danbridge said.

'If you want to be formal, *Mister Councilman*.'

The laughter that followed was easy. There was no awkwardness between the pair. They had known each other for too long to let something like official titles stand between them.

They fell in to walk beside each other, feeling the rising heat of the new day. In a little while Telegraph Hill would be simmering under the full extent of the Texas sun. Glancing down Clem saw his boots were already showing a faint mist of fine dust. Nothing he could do about that, Clem thought with a slight ripple of irritation.

They walked along main street, Clem aware of the curious heads showing in store doorways as he passed. They were all known to him. All good friends. And the people who, for the most part, had voted for him.

There were calls of *good luck, Clem.* Other congratulations. Even one from Sam Brinker who had been Clem's rival for the post of lawman.

'I'll leave you to get settled in,' Danbridge said as they reached the bank building.

As they parted company Clem continued along the street, exchanging pleasantries with passersby. He saw the law office just ahead. A stone and timber building that offered a permanent reminder of Telegraph Hill's solidarity as a community.

There were barred windows either side of the oak door with its own smaller window set in the wood. To the left of the door was the shingle that announced: *Marshal's Office–Telegraph Hill–Texas.* The boardwalk outside the building was clean swept. That would be down to Lucas Berryman, official deputy for the town.

Berryman had been deputy for over six years, under Hank Warren. Warren had worn the badge of marshal for a long time and had finally turned it in due to reaching his sixtieth birthday. He had figured he was due a rest and decided to retire and move to Lubbock and spend time with his widowed sister on her small ranch.

It had been Warren who had persuaded Clem to run for office. Clem had always been civic minded and once word got around he was considering the position, a vociferous campaign had been mounted. Sam Brinker had put himself up against Clem and their rivalry had been strong but friendly. Clem won by a landslide. Brinker had been the first to shake Clem's hand.

Clem paused at the door, not hesitating for too long in case people were watching. He pushed the door open and stepped inside. The generous office, cooler inside because the thick stone walls kept most of the heat out. The first thing he was aware of was the smell of coffee from the enamel pot on the stove. Marshal Warren had kept the pot heating all day.

Clem took a look around the office. The cell block to his left, big desk on the right facing the cells. A couple of wooden file cabinets against the wall. The newly fitted telephone fixed near them, and the chained gun rack on the wall behind the desk. It held a number of Winchester rifles and a pair of Greener shotguns. Under the rack a narrow shelf held a store of ammuni-

tion and a hook on the wall beside the rack supported the gunrig and .45 caliber Colt Peacemaker Warren had carried during the years he had been marshal. He had only had to use the weapon three times in anger.

For the second time that morning a fleeting memory scooted across Clem's mind. Of another time and place he'd allowed to fade.

Warren's high-backed swivel chair stood behind the desk. It had a cover of dark leather, always kept clean and polished and Clem could see Warren seated there as he worked on the paperwork that came with the job. He had never been happy when it came to dealing with the paperwork. He would have rather been out about town dealing with people.

On the wall to one side of the desk a notice board held pinned flyers. Town ordinance declarations and a scattering of wanted posters. Tucked in the corner of the office was the smaller desk used by Berryman. He was there now, bent over some paperwork of his own and he looked up as Clem stepped inside, closing the door behind him.

Lucas Berryman was in his early thirties. He looked younger, with his rounded face and the thick fall of hair. Standing he reached just under six feet, with good shoulders and a rangy build.

'Morning, Clem ... I mean *Marshal Tatum*.'

He stood, reaching out a big hand to shake Clem's.

'We've known each other long enough, Lucas. You call me Clem unless we have company.'

Berryman ducked his head. 'You're the boss.'

'Anything I need to deal with that's urgent?'

'Town's pretty quiet. Like it mostly is I guess.'

'You won't find me complaining about that.'

Clem hung his hat from one of the wall hooks, took a walk across the office to glance through the bars at the three empty cells.

'We had a couple punchers from the Bar-X in there yesterday, had a mite too much to drink over at the *Crystal Palace*. Made a lot of noise but nothing else. I herded them up and put 'em in the cells. Let 'em out first thing this morning. You missed 'em by a half hour.' Berryman took a sheet of paper from his desk. 'I wrote it all up for the files. Marshal Warren liked to keep everything neat and tidy.'

'Well, we can keep that up, Lucas. You can take me through the paperwork later.'

'You want some coffee?'

Clem nodded. 'Be good,' he said.

He crossed to where the gunrig hung from the wall and took it down. He slid out the pistol and placed it on his desk. Took of his coat and put on the belt and holster, adjusting it until he felt comfortable. He picked up the

pistol, a .45 caliber Colt Peacemaker, the blued steel smooth and shiny, self-conscious as he checked the load, making sure the hammer rested on an empty chamber.

'Wouldn't do to go and shoot myself in the foot,' he said.

'You're going to do fine,' Berryman said.

Clem glanced his way. 'If I don't a lot of people are going to be disappointed.'

He slipped on his coat again, letting the skirt cover most of the holstered gun.

Berryman had filled two china mugs from the pot and handed one to Clem. They stood in silence. Drinking slowly.

The clock on the wall made its presence know, the ticking sound as solid as the walls of the jail as Clem sat at the desk and settled in to deal with the paperwork in front of him. It held no problems for him. Being the owner of a store paperwork was a familiar chore.

**

A couple of hours later Clem pushed aside the papers and stood.

'I guess I'd better show my face around town,' he said.

'I got this paperwork to finish,' Berryman said. 'Can't keep putting it off.'

Clem picked up his hat and set it squarely on his head. Moved to the door.

Stepping outside he felt the rising heat. Tasted the faint haze of dust from a passing rider. Across the street, a couple of doors down he could see the store he owned and ran with Ari. A hardware emporium that served the town as it had for a number of years. Clem's late father had opened the place soon after he and his son had arrived in Telegraph Hill. Clem couldn't see his wife but he knew she would be watching him through the big display window with its gilded sign across the glass. He felt the need to move, turning along the boardwalk and heading up town.

The feel of the holstered pistol felt heavy against his hip. Something he would need to get used to. As he would the recognition he was receiving from people as he passed by. Clem took the time to make himself known. He showed himself in store doorways, giving a brief nod and word. He felt the need to make himself known to the people he now served even though he knew them all by name.

Telegraph Hill was a nice town. Growing stronger. New businesses opening. More people arriving. Civic amenities appearing. Talk of laying a new surface along Main Street, if ever the town council could finally make the decision. A growing number of telephones in use in business premises and homes. The fire station had been opened three months back. The restaurant he passed refurbished by its new owners.

Clem took it in with a fresh perspective. More than before this was *his* town. And now it was his responsibility.

He watched the street traffic. Wagons. Private buggies. A number of horsemen moving the length of the wide, dusty street. A group of five taking a slow canter as they rode from west to east. He didn't recognize them. They were dressed in range clothes. Looked as if they had been riding for some time. Hands from one of the local spreads? After all it was Friday. The day when Telegraph Hill welcomed hands come to enjoy themselves after a week's work, though most wouldn't show until later in the afternoon.

At the extreme end of the street Clem crossed over to begin his return journey. Stopped to have a word with Dan Pauly, owner of the livery stable. Pauly was in his fifties, lean and brown from the sun.

'They say it gets easier as time goes by,' Pauly said.

'They do?'

'Clem, I'll tell you something now. Your dad would have been proud to see you today.'

'I hope so. Six years since he passed and I still miss him, Dan.'

Pauly patted his shoulder. 'Hell, son, we all do, and that's a fact.'

'See you later, Dan.'

Clem crossed the street and started

his walk on the opposite side. As he drew level with the *Crystal Palace* saloon, Rafe Jackson the owner-operator stepped outside and nodded to him.

Jackson was a big man, as wide as he was broad. Mutton-chop sideburns reached as far as his double-chins.

'Starting as you mean to go on?'

'The people voted me in to watch over the town, Rafe. It's what I get paid to do.'

'I guess so.' Jackson shielded his eyes as he looked skyward. 'Don't envy you walkin' up and down in this heat. Looks like it's goin' to be a long, hot one.'

Clem realized wearing his coat had been a mistake. He took it off and draped it across his left arm.

'I'll drop this off at the store,' he said.

'Clem, that's a pure excuse to go visit that pretty wife of yours.'

'Never crossed my mind,' he said.

Leaving the saloon Clem walked into the store and hung his coat on a hook behind the counter, bidding hello to a couple of customers. Ari appeared, smiling when she saw him.

'Tired of the new job already,' she said. Teasing him with the special tone only she could use. 'Taking refuge in here?'

'I think I'll last the day.'

Even later, when he thought about, Clem never figured out what made him take out the holstered Colt and add that sixth bullet, Ari's eyes on him. She said nothing at first. When he started for the door she touched his arm.

'I told Nathanial I'd collect him at lunch time. I promised to take him to the café as a special treat being your first day.'

'Then I will make it part of my route to look out for you both,' Clem said.

'He'll like that. Clem, be careful.'

Clem kissed her on the cheek. Walked out of the store and continued his tour, making himself known to the people of Telegraph Hill.

**

Hoyt Gage took his beer and joined his four partners at a table close to the saloon's front window. From there he was able to view Main Street. And one building in particular. The *Crystal Palace* was quiet at this time in the morning. Only a few customers idling away the late morning.

If he had not had other things occupying his mind Gage would have appreciated the saloon's finer points. The interior was well appointed, with polished oak bar and brass fittings. Gleaming mirror behind the bar and rows of bottles lined up. It was maintained at a high level and in Telegraph Hill it had a good reputation. A reputation Rafe Jackson had worked hard to achieve.

Standing behind the long bar he found he was studying the five men occupying the front window table. He couldn't put his finger on why, but they made him a tad uneasy. Outwardly they hadn't done anything to cause him concern. Just a bunch of men stopping off for a cooling beer, talking between themselves. They were roughly dressed in what Jackson termed range clothes, looking as if they had just come off a cattle drive, though one was clad in a long duster. Jackson folded and refolded a clean bar towel as he casually watched them. When he realized he was folding the towel again he pushed it aside and moved along the bar, watching the men in the large mirror behind him.

Settle down, Rafe, he told himself. *They just came in for a beer. You're acting like an old woman. They ain't done anything wrong.*

He started as the batwings swung open and a couple of his regulars came in, deep in conversation. Realized it was reaching close on noon and the place would soon fill up.

More customers began to filter in, the saloon buzzing with conversation and Jackson became busy. Yet he couldn't rid his mind of the five men.

Through the window he saw the town's new lawman, Clem Tatum, on the far side of the street, walking by. He found he had an urge to call out to him but his train of thought was broken as voices reached from his waiting customers.

**

The town clock, mounted above the town hall, began to chime out midday. Main Street was quieting down as people headed for lunch, either in restaurants or going home. A normal Friday in Telegraph Hill.

Clem saw his deputy standing outside the jail and raised a quick hand as he passed. He had spent the last couple of hours in conversation with the residents of Telegraph Hill, listening to their concerns and their congratulations, and was fast realizing just what being the resident lawman meant.

At the end of the street Clem spotted Ari and his son walking from the schoolhouse. He increased his pace as he moved to meet them.

A normal day in Telegraph Hill that was about to change and be remembered for a long time afterwards ...

**

The five men in the saloon drained their beer and casually rose, sauntering out the door. They took their horses and walked them across the street, in no particular hurry. They crossed the over at an angle, taking themselves in the direction of the bank.

There was no hitch rail outside that building so they tethered their mounts just up from it. One man, Dan Forrester, stood with the horses to make sure they stayed quiet, while Hoyt Gage led his bunch directly to the bank. None of them carried any weapon apart from the pistols holstered at their hips, except for Lester Sandoval, who had a Greener carried under his long duster. They didn't want to attract too much attention as they went inside.

**

There were three tellers in position. Henry Danbridge had just left his office in conversation with a client. They were part way across the floor when Gage and his three partners stepped inside. One man closed the door and stood with his back to it.

On Gage's nod guns were drawn, Sandoval's shotgun making its presence known. There was no need for orders to be given. They had done this kind of thing before and knew the procedure.

'No noise,' Gage said. 'Do anything stupid and we *will* kill you. Simple as that. Don't believe me you'll find out the hard way. We just want the money. Paper. No coins.'

The tall, whip thin Cal Tessler pulled a couple of folded cloth bags from his pants and tossed them on the counter in front of the tellers.

'*Fill 'em,*' he said. 'Empty all the drawers.'

Gage turned his handgun on Danbridge 'You the boss man? Open the safe and show me what you got in there.' When Danbridge hesitated he said, 'You get one chance at this. You want to die for pieces of paper?'

Danbridge, as much as he liked money, liked life better and moved to do as he was told. The thick safe doors revealed even more cash.

'Jim, fill your bags,' Gage said.

Jim Rains took out the cloth sacks he carried and began to pack in stacks of bills.

Gage saw that the tellers had emptied their drawers. He waved his gun at them.

'Out from behind the counter. Down on the floor and stay still.'

Sandoval, watching through the window, said, 'Lookin' quiet, Hoyt.'

'It's a quiet town. Why I picked it,' Gage said. 'You boys done? Okay, we go. Straight to the horses and ride out. Try and keep it steady.'

They gathered at the door. Gage caught Forrester's eye and he gave a nod of understanding, freeing reins and holding the bunched horses.

They moved along the boardwalk, loose bunched and scanning the street around them. This was not their first robbery. They knew this was the time things could go wrong. The quiet before a possible storm.

They might have made it if Henry Danbridge hadn't appeared in the bank door, courage returning, and yelling with enough force to reach

Art by Alexandre Koyama

across the street.

'*They robbed the bank. Stop them somebody ...*'

Sandoval, bringing up the rear, turned about. The Greener he carried swung up. Sandoval pulled the first trigger. The shot from the barrel spat out a gout of flame and smoke. The charge didn't have space enough to spread. The main shot blasted the gilded glass of the bank door, spraying it about and tearing at the timber frame. Henry Danbridge caught the edge of the shot. Lead tore at his expensive jacket and ripped into the flesh of his right arm. He was twisted by the force of the shot, too shocked to make any more sound as he stumbled and hit the door frame, legs giving under him. He pitched to the boardwalk.

**

After seconds of nothing the sound of a woman screaming broke the silence. Heads turned in the direction of the gunshot.

Clem registered the shotgun blast, dropped his hand to the butt of his holstered pistol as he swiveled his head in the direction of the sound.

'*Clem..?*' Ari said.

He made a grab for her arm, wanting to get her and Nathanial off the street. Fear clutched at his insides as he realized he and his family were close to the five men. Too close.

'*Pa,*' Nathanial said and there was genuine fear in his words now.

Clem saw he and his family were alone in the middle of the street with no immediate cover.

Out the corner of his eye Clem saw Berryman turn about and rush inside the jail.

Then a crackle of gunfire rolled through the hot air as the bunched men on the boardwalk started to fire. Bullets made angry sounds as they were fired in every direction, more as a distraction while the robbers made for their horses.

And then Clem heard Ari give an abrupt cry. She faltered and went to her knees. A surge of blood spread across her dress, over her ribs.

'*Get down, Nate. Stay with your ma.*'

Clem's .45 was in his hand and he raised his arm, leveling the weapon, hammer going back. He had to push the image of Ari falling out of his mind as he found a target, held it before squeezing back on the trigger. He felt the Colt buck in his hand.

Col Tessler stumbled as the solid impact of the slug hit him in the chest. He fell back against the building behind him. A hoarse moan burst from his lips. The gun in his hand went off, the bullet splintering the boardwalk at his feet. After that the gun slipped from his hand as his strength faded. He didn't know it but the .45 slug had gone all the way through and blown out of his spine. His suddenly lifeless legs gave way under him and he dropped loosely to the boardwalk.

Clem forced himself to stay focused. On the fringe of his vision he saw townsfolk scattering. Thankfully there were only a few on the street.

The thought crowded his mind.

My first day. Not even a full one. This can't be happening ...

But it was and he had to deal with it.

**

Hoyt Gage read it in the same way. For him this was pure survival now. It should have been easy. Telegraph Hill was no wide open, hell-for-leather town. It was supposed to have been a sleepy burg. Easy for the taking.

He saw the lawdog, star on his vest, gun in his hand. Standing firm in the middle of the street, covering the wounded woman and the boy.

Sonofabitch had already put Col down.

Gage turned his own gun in the lawman's direction.

Jim Rains yelled out.

'Deputy with a shotgun.'

Lucas Berryman had run out from the jail, shotgun in his hands and he kept moving, crossing the street to cut in their direction.

Hammers back he leveled the weapon, triggering at the man at-

49

tempting to control the milling horses, startled by the gunfire.

When Berryman fired, the charge clipped Forrester's left hip. He let go the reins and the bunched horses reared away, turning in different directions as they scattered across the street, raising dust.

Clem had to pull aside as one animal almost slammed into him. He lost his balance, skidding to his knees, spitting rising dust out of his mouth.

When he was able to see again the men on the boardwalk were moving apart, guns firing as they separated.

Rains had come off the boardwalk, clutching his handgun as he picked up on Clem. He still held a sack of bank money in his left hand.

'I ain't quitting this town 'til I kill me a lawdog,' he said.

His gun lanced flame and smoke.

Clem felt the solid punch of the bullet hitting his left arm high up. It jolted him but there was no pain at first.

Rains showed a wide grin when he saw he had shot Clem. He dogged back his hammer for a second try. One he never made.

Clem had brought his own gun on line and fired a single shot that took Rains in the throat. He gave a shrill cry, head going back and blood bursting from the ragged wound, washing down his shirt front.

The solid boom of Berryman's shotgun sent its second burst into Forrester's mid-section, opening him up in a scatter of bloody innards.

**

Rafe Jackson rushed out of the *Crystal Palace*, white apron flapping. He carried a long-barreled shotgun in his hands as he homed in on Sandoval, who was fumbling a fresh cartridge into his Greener to replace one he had fired. If he had used the one remaining he might have stood a chance. But he wanted to have both barrels full again, and it was his undoing. He saw Jackson running in his direction and in his haste he dropped the shell and tried to close the shotgun. Jackson offered him no chance.

He leveled the weapon he carried and triggered his first barrel. The charge caught Sandoval dead center, tearing into his body and shredded his clothing and flesh in an instant. Sandoval had a startled expression on his face as the impact of the shot lifted him off his feet and literally threw him against the bank window. The glass caved under him, Sandoval spinning over the sill in a flash of blood. He crashed to the floor of the bank, his Greener loose in his hands as he landed.

**

Behind him Clem heard Ari's voice and it took every part of his being to ignore her as he swung his Colt around to line up on the last of the group. He didn't know the man's name was Hoyt Gage, a man with a violent past, now on his own as his men were all down.

As far as Clem Tatum was concerned Gage was simply a criminal who had come into Telegraph Hill with the sole intention of robbing the bank and deserved what was happening to him and his crew.

And being the town's official lawman it was Clem's job to stop him.

The seconds between the pair seemed to stretch as they eyed each other.

The outlaw and the marshal.

Neither willing to concede.

Clem allowed a moment of thinking what Gage had done in Telegraph Hill. Not just to the town but to Clem's own wife, and it was that more than anything guiding his hand.

Gage's Colt flashed in the sunlight as he brought it to bear on the already bloodied lawman. His finger stroked back on the trigger, the hammer dropping and the muzzle spitting flame and smoke. He saw Clem stagger as the bullet burned against his right hip and realized he had fired too fast. He thumbed back the hammer for

a follow-up shot.

He never made it.

Clem had steadied his right arm,

grip firm as he held his target. Tripped the trigger, cocked and fired again, and a third time, placing all three shots in Gage's chest. Solid, killing shots that gouted blood, and sent Gage staggering back as they drove him down. There was a finality in Clem's actions as he adjusted his aim and put his remaining shot into Gage's forehead, dropping him to the street.

**

People began to crowd the street. Telegraph Hill's doctor, Miles Swanton appeared, and commandeered assistance to take Ari and Henry Danbridge to his office. By this time Clem was at her side, ignoring his blood-soaked arm and hip as he shuffled towards the doctor's office. He had given orders to Berryman to oversee the aftermath of the robbery and deal with concerns of the town, promising to be back to help as soon as he could.

In Doc Swanson's surgery the town medic went about his business with the calm and proficiency he was known for. His wife, Saundra, who acted as his nurse assistant, saw to Ari because Clem made such a fuss the only way to quiet him down was for her to deal with Ari first.

Swanson had his hands full with Clem and Henry Dandridge. His initial examination confirmed that the banker had the lesser injury and quickly bound his arm with a thick bandage before turning his attention to Clem. It took him some time to stop the blood from his arm as he removed the bullet and saw to the wound. The bullet to Clem's hip had gone clean through, clipping bone and muscle. It was a wound that was going to take time to heal and even though it did Clem was left with a slight limp and forced him to use a cane when it sometimes bothered him – though it didn't plague him enough to have to quit as Telegraph Hill's lawman, the post he kept for many years.

Ari's injury kept her chair-bound for a number of days. She had lost blood and it left her weak. She was determined not to allow herself become an invalid, her concern more for Clem and seeing that young Nathanial didn't suffer any after effects. That turned out to be nothing to worry about. With the resilience of youth he bounced back from his experience quickly, becoming something of a celebrity among his peers for having been there, on the spot, when Clem Tatum defeated the Hoyt Gage gang of bank robbers.

Clem played down the incident. He had not been as alone as some would have it. His Deputy Lucas Berryman had played his part and so had Rafe Jackson, the saloon keeper.

Despite his protestations Clem became the hero of the hour. Telegraph

Hill's lawman shooter. Wielding his gun in the face of overwhelming odds and putting down the infamous Gage Bunch. In the local saloons the story was expanded and embellished with each telling and Clem himself, once he was able to move around again, was feted by everyone he met.

Yet Clem, despite being asked on many occasions how he showed his skill with his gun, merely shrugged

and said in the heat of the moment he simply did what was expected of him and left it at that.

It left questions unanswered and for the most part as time went by were forgotten.

Except by Ari Tatum, who saw her husband in a different light, and persisted with her feminine wiles, questioning and probing as to why the husband she imagined she knew so well had revealed on that day a side totally alien to her.

**

Sitting on the verandah on a quiet, sun-dappled afternoon a week after the incident, Ari glanced at him, watched as he flexed his leg as the lingering ache persisted.

'You saved Nate and me and for that I will always love you. You defended the town and you faced those men with a skill I never once imagined you possessed. You may have fooled Telegraph Hill Clem Tatum, but not me. I hope we have a long and happy life together but I will keep on asking until I know the truth, so either tell me, or I *will* pester you every one of those days.'

It was not the first time she had raised the subject. Now Clem might have been able to fend off the curiosity of the townsfolk but Ari was not so easily dealt with.

'Before dad and I came to Telegraph Hill we lived way back on the Cimarron Strip. This was before it became the Oklahoma Panhandle. Me, my ma and pa. Small spread with a few cattle. Some farmland. There was town close enough by. Ma died suddenly when I was fifteen years old. She never had been a healthy woman. Left just me and my pa. Day we buried ma I saw pa talking with the local part-time sheriff. Name of Dan Valance. Tall man who wore a big pistol on his left hip. Something about that gun fascinated me. When I asked pa about him later he kind of brushed me off. Didn't want to speak about it. A couple of weeks after there was a shooting in town and I heard that Valance had been shot and killed by a man called Nate Cunningham. It appeared Cunningham had been a gunman. Had killed a number of men. Appeared he was very fast and accurate with his gun. When pa heard about the shooting he went all quiet. It was scary. Pa was no coward. He faced everything in his life head on. But hearing about Cunningham really put him on edge. I remember the day after Valance's funeral he saddled

his horse and went to town. Just told me to sit tight and wait for him to come back ...'

Clem broke off and wandered inside the house. When he came back he held a bottle of beer in his hand, the glass still cool and frosted from the ice box. He sat down again and took a drink, staring out across the verandah.

'... you have to remember at that time on the strip, the Cimarron was real rough territory. Wild and open with little real law. Our town had been lucky to have Valance. He and pa were good friends. Been so for many years. But this man Cunningham, a gunman, *pistolero*, whatever you want to call him, was a bad man. Folk were scared of him. Walked around him and kept their mouths closed. I figure shooting Valance had been easy for him. He added it to his list of killings. My pa, the tale went, rode into town and faced up to Cunningham, called him out and when Cunningham went for his gun Pa drew and shot him dead. Folk who saw it said Cunningham never even got his gun clear of the holster. When pa drew it was so fast it was over before anyone realized he'd even pulled his gun. Thing is until that day I never even knew pa had a gun, let alone knew how to use it.'

'But your pa was the quietest, gentlest man I ever knew,' Ari said, thinking back. 'Kept to himself living in that house outside of town.'

Clem nodded in agreement.

'He once told me a man has nothing to prove to anyone as long as he's true to himself. After he shot Cunningham he took me aside and told me about his life before he met ma. He had been something of a wild younker. Took to the gun and taught himself how to handle it better than most. For a few years he had a reputation that he couldn't rid himself of. Until he met the two people who influenced his life. One was Dan Valance. The other was my ma. Between them they turned pa around. Made him put away his gun and build his family life.

'After pa shot Cunningham he realized things could get bad again, so he sold the spread and we left town without saying a word to anyone. Spent some time simply drifting around, pa taking work whenever he could find it. He was pretty handy at most things and we did pretty well. By the time I was seventeen we'd moved this way and when pa reached Telegraph Hill he really took to it. We had enough money saved from selling the old spread and added to it from the work pa and I did to buy the general store in town. Wasn't much at first but we worked hard and made a go of it.'

Ari watched him sup his beer. Knew there was more, but waited until he was ready to tell it.

'While we were on the trail during those years pa took out his gun one day. He'd never showed it to me before and I understood the time would come when he was ready. I never forgot that day he handed me the rig and told me to put it on, adjusted the way it hung for me. Took out that pistol and loaded it ...

'You're of an age now, Clem. Time you learned how to handle this thing. Now heed me, boy, 'cause if you even think about the wrong way of it you and*

me is going to fall out. Gun is a means of protecting yourself. It's not there so you can show how smart you are with it. I near to ruined my life thinking that. I was lucky. Two people showed me what a damn fool I was and I hid away that gun until the day I used it to put down Nate Cunningham after he shot Dan Valance. Since that day I never wore it again. Just kept it clean and oiled because I knew the time would come when I needed to school you.'

Rufus Tatum held the blued Colt .45 in his hand and for a moment he drifted back to the days he had worn it and enjoyed the feeling it gave him. He eased the hammer back so he could spin the cylinder and a wistful expression clouded his eyes. Then he felt Clem's gaze fixed on him and remembered what he was doing.

'A gun can take hold of you. Make you feel ten foot tall and indestructible. I never want that for you. Ain't no glamour in what a bullet can do to a man and some of those things are worse than just dyin'. You take note, Clem, and hope you never have to see those things.

'I'll show you how to handle one of these pistols and you take it in and remember.

'You never take that gun out unless you mean to use it. If that happens remember one thing – one that can save you. When you face a man remember he's going to try and kill you. No two ways about it. You have a split second to decide whether you want to live or die. If you make the wrong choice it's likely going to be over for you and the other feller gets to walk away. Keep that in mind, boy. Now you may never need to face another gun, but if you do just re-

call what I'm saying.'

'He made me practice with that gun every day out on the trail with an empty cylinder. Drawing and firing. Drawing and firing until it became as natural as pulling breath. More concerned with aiming than being too fast. Taking that extra moment to fix my target. Told me that it was the man who hit his target rather than the quickest to pull a trigger. A month before he allowed me a loaded gun. Made me wait that extra second so I had my target fixed in my mind. Weird thing was it worked. I found I was hitting more times than not. Pa made me promise not to talk about what I'd learned. Said those lessons would come back if I found myself in the right situation. Now when we reached Telegraph Hill he took away that gun and I never saw it again, but those thing he taught me were stuck in my mind. When I faced those men outside the bank pa's words came back. Like he was there reminding me. Ari, I only had two things on my mind. You and Nate. That you had been hurt and you were both in danger. I needed to do something about it.'

She touched his hand. Fingers cool on his skin.

'And you did, Clem. You saved us both and dealt with those men. And remember what they did to you. You were hurt, Clem, but you saved the town as well. Don't you ever forget that because Telegraph Hill won't.'

Clem saw a figure move into view on the street, heading their way. It was Henry Danbridge. The banker still had his arm in a sling, held against his body. He touched the brim of his hat as he drew level with Clem's house.

'How are you both, Ari?'

Ari smiled. 'Better each day, Henry. And you?'

'Grateful to be alive. Thanks to Clem. Now when will Marshal Tatum be able to take up his position again?'

'Most likely tomorrow,' Clem said. 'A little stiff but at least I can sit behind my desk and let Lucas do the legwork for a while.'

'Town's asking about you most every day. They're impatient to see their hero on his feet again.' Dandridge glanced at Ari. 'You have a good man there, Ari Tatum.

Ari colored but held his gaze. 'Oh, I know that, Henry. I know that.' She turned her head and looked across at Clem. 'I know that more than most ...'

'Then I will see you in the morning Clem – *Marshal Tatum.'*

Danbridge continued his slow walk along the street.

Heading for town.

Passing the sign that said Telegraph Hill. A new legend had been carved in the wood. It stated the simple legend:

The Site Of The Killing At Telegraph Hill.

THE 'SAUERKRAUT' WESTERN

Spotlighting Alfred Wallon's continuing campaign to keep the western alive and well in Germany.

Alfred Wallon has always been an avid reader. Born on May 20, 1957 in Marburg, Germany, and raised in a nearby village, his love of the written word began when he first entered school and discovered comics. Alfred's other great passion, however, was always the western.

By the early 1980s, he was writing them for a number of publishers. In addition, this prolific wordsmith has also written fantasy and romance novels, as well as many entries in the ever-popular Kommissar X series.

But his first allegiance remains to the western—indeed, he also continues to work tirelessly to promote the genre.

"William W. Johnstone always assured his readers that the West would live on as long as he did," says the author, "and I feel the same way myself. While ever I can write westerns, the Old West will never die."

In Germany, the western genre has become a niche product for the major publishing houses. Most decision-makers at top management level have now turned to other genres. One reason for this is that they come from a different generation: in other words, they didn't grow up with the Western, and therefore have no great knowledge or understanding of the genre ... or its continuing appeal to fans.

Fortunately, there are still smaller publishers who see the situation very differently and want to save some of the forgotten treasures of the last 50 years, especially in the western genre. One publisher in particular has already proven this point quite successfully for more than three years. We are talking about the eBook publisher, Edition Bärenklau.

"In 2015 I asked Alfred Wallon if we could publish his western novels, which had over the previous thirty-five years, been issued by various other publishers," explains Jörg Munsonius, owner of Edition Bärenklau. "This led to further opportunities for closer cooperation."

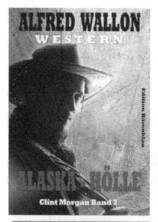

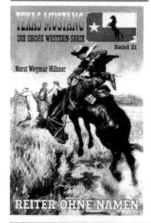

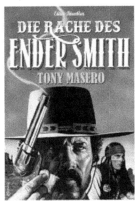

Alfred Wallon himself continues, "Jörg Munsonius asked me if I would become head of the Western and Adventure Department at Edition Bärenklau. It was an idea I loved, because I've read more than a thousand westerns over the last 40 years and have also established contacts with various fellow writers during this time. I knew immediately which authors I wanted to address, and did exactly that."

In the last three years, Edition Bärenklau has significantly expanded the western range. Well-known 'home-grown' authors such as Glenn Stirling, John F. Beck, Larry Lash, Heinz Squarra and Horst W. Hübner are represented with their entire life's work at Edition Bärenklau.

"We've published several hundred Westerns in the last three years," says Munsonius. "And we're confident that this number will increase significantly in the coming years. Meanwhile we have the largest and most diverse western program in the eBook sector in Germany—even though we are actually only a small publisher. But we know which authors are worth publishing."

Meanwhile Edition Bärenklau is also publishing German-language editions of English and American Westerns. Authors include Ben Bridges and Tony Masero, and Piccadilly Publishing's very own Edward Martin has also provided cover art to make sure the books stand out from the competition.

Translations of American authors are also planned. A recent contract was signed with Linda Pendleton, wife of the legendary author Don Pendleton, for an extensive book package. This includes novels by Linda and *The Executioner* novels by Don.

"All the signs point to expansion," states Wallon. "While the big publishing houses no longer know how to handle good Western novels, we know our product and we know our market. Of course, intensive research on the Internet, an exchange with fellow collectors and contacts with the authorities are necessary. We have extended our lead here and our publications clearly demonstrate the diversity of the Western genre. With this in mind, we want to continue."

In detail, the program contains to publish the works and series of well-known German authors, or the works from the post-war period from 1950 onwards, where it has become difficult to clarify the legal situation.

Among the early publications are the books of Larry Lash, the pseudonym of the author Bernhard Boemke, who published between 250-270 novels in the field of the Wild West novel.

Another, younger example is Florian Beck, who published more than 500 novels as John F. Beck. Another great author of the 1970s to 1990s was Heinz Squarra, alias H. S. Sharon.

Of course, there were even more big western authors and series with high sales, but they deserve their own article. It is worth mentioning that in these decades, series periodicals were also published—single novels published week after week, which often ran to 500-1500 issues.

Also worth mentioning for the Munsonius and Wallon is the great western saga RONCO, which ran a staggering 493 issues between April 1972 and September 1982, and the SILVER WESTERN series, which started in 1952 and ended with volume 1903 in 1996. Here, too, we would need an article all of its own to really do justice to these series.

So many lost treasures have been discovered by "Edition Bärenklau" and made accessible to a growing but still manageable audience. The publishing house and head of department have set themselves this great job for the next several years.

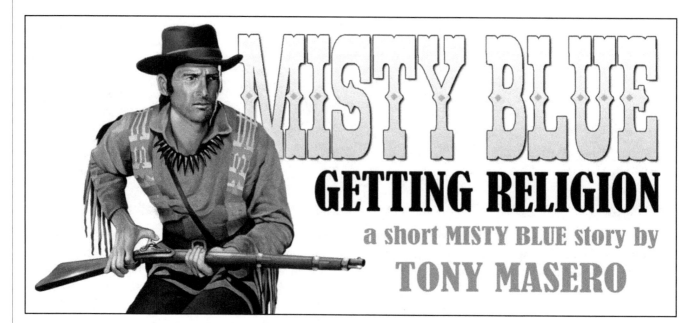

MISTY BLUE
GETTING RELIGION
a short MISTY BLUE story by
TONY MASERO

S ome say he was a trader's son, their post stationed at a fork of the Missouri and Yellowstone. The owner, his father, favored trade with the Mountain Men who would come down to sell their furs and debauch themselves when the season was over. It is told the boy was one of fourteen children and for want of interest and divertissement he would often spend time with a band of Sioux Indians encamped nearby and so learnt their ways and skills.

Hugh Glass, that famed bear-mauled trapper, gives report in having been there at the trading post and tells of the young lad so keen and eager to hear more of life in the yonder. It was himself, so Glass claims, that gave the boy the name he bears. For never had he seen such a youngster go so misty-eyed at the tales of high adventure and perilous danger in the distant Rocky Mountains that he shared with the boy around the evening fireside.

That would have been back in the year of 1832 and it took another nine years for the seed that Glass planted in the young boy's mind to come to fruition. For then at the age of nineteen years, the said Misty Blue quit his home to make his own way in the world.

A fit and sturdy young man, full six foot one and half inches tall and weighing in at two hundred pounds of bone and sinew, he had all that befitted a man of fortitude and was well suited for the life of a Mountain Man.

His adventures were many and recorded elsewhere, how he served as scout, searched for gold, be a hunter, tracker, whiskey peddler and guide. But those days were behind him and in the year 1867 he descended from his lone exile in the mountains and returned to that wasteland below that some men called civilization.

M isty Blue spread the letter out flat on the cluttered tavern table. He carefully pressed over the folded edges and eased the bends and creases so he might see it better in the poor candlelight. Misty stared at it a long time, toying with the necklace of bear claws that his now dead Shoshoni woman had given him for protection. He scrubbed at his unshaven jaw as he pondered over the missive.

The owner of the establishment wandered across, he was a well-built fellow, nay, more than that, he was fat and gloriously so. Around his bountiful midriff he wore a canvas apron stretched and laced as tight as a virgin spinster's corset. His face was round like a pie and his button eyes merely raisins in the crust.

'Can I serve you more, fellow?' he asked, doubtful that this buckskin clad figure had the wherewithal for another jug.

'You can,' said Misty without looking up. 'That is if you can read.'

'I can indeed,' said the tavern keeper proudly. 'I have both letters and numbers, my first wife taught me so.'

Misty raised an eyebrow, 'And how many have you had?'

The keeper chuckled jovially, 'Wives? Why, seven it is at last count. I have dipped frequently at the well, as they say.'

'They must have fed you right well too,' Misty observed.

'So they did and here you see the result,' he answered slapping both hands on his belly with a glow of contentment. 'I am, sir, as you will see, a man of most prodigious appetite,' he closed one of his small peepers in a wink.

'Then I just hope your bucket matches the wellhead. So tell me? Will you read this letter for me?'

The innkeeper licked his lips and his pig eyes narrowed into a thin squint of calculation, 'We have charges for such things, letter writing and reading, postage and accounting.'

'I will pay,' Misty agreed. 'Although—' he paused a moment in consideration. 'If it is bad news I might change my mind.'

'Then pay me now, for I know not what you have there.'

Searching in the satchel he carried, Misty threw coin on the table, 'Take what you will from that and read me what it says.'

The innkeeper scooped coin from the table and picked up the letter, dipping it so he might see better against the candlelight for the tavern was a dim place without any windows. He scanned the letter quickly and with some interest whilst Misty waited impatiently.

'My, my,' the innkeeper muttered. 'Tut-tut,' he went.

His studious consideration drew the attention of others in the inn and soon a curious crowd was gathered around. Many of them were men of the mountains and like Misty were often starved of human contact so that any interest of a social kind was sought after and shared.

'Come then, fellow,' urged an eager voice from amongst the audience 'Let us hear.'

'It is from a sister of the church,' the innkeeper began.

That raised Misty's eyebrows, 'A nun, you say?'

'Aye, Sister Winifred of the Convent of Lesser Sorrows.'

'And how did it come here?'

'There are addresses on the envelope, it seems to have taken quite a journey,' the ales-man informed him. 'From one Abner Blue, in Target Town—'

'My brother,' Misty acknowledged.

'A certain Etta Jane—'

'Ah, yes,' sighed Misty, remembering the girl's mother with fondness. 'Then this is definitely from a little sister of mine, for of a certain she took the veil. Proceed.'

'Indeed so, she writes it thus: *Dearest Brother, it is my entire wish that this letter reach you and finds you safe in the hands of God.*'

Misty Blue, who was not a conventional believer being a man who worshiped more at Nature's altar than under any roof, nodded appreciation at the thought nonetheless. 'Go on,' he said.

'*I was no more than a small child when you set off to make your way amongst the distant hills, confronting beasts and wild savages so I am sure you will find it strange that I write to you so. Word reaches us here of your exploits and, although I am timorous to do so, Reverend Mother has suggested this communication and I take up pen and paper to obey her instruction—*'

One old hoary listener leaned forward curiously, 'What's that word '*tremonrus*'? What's that mean?'

'Like you, dimwit,' chimed in another. 'A scaredy-pants.'

'No, no,' said the innkeeper in a haughty instructive tone. 'It means more like 'timid', 'fearful', as a small mouse might be.'

'I thought you said she was a nun now she's a *mouse*?' barked the first.

'Will you shut your gab,' snarled Misty. 'Read on, man and forget the subtitles.'

'*We are beset here in the Convent by a most troubling affair and we trust you may be able to help us in this time of trial. We sisters are very content in*

our religious community, there are no more than five of us Sisters of Lesser Sorrow and we occupy a nunnery that has attached to it a stretch of land that has come into dispute. A certain local rancher has confronted us with an altercation as he claims ownership. The land is rich and we grow the crops there that sustain us so to lose it would mean certain closure of our Convent.'

'I'm befuddled by that word '*alteration*', what kind of alteration might that be?' interrupted the same old gray beard.

'I said '*altercation*' not alteration,' corrected the innkeeper.

'Yeah, but—'

Misty, tiring of the annoying interruptions reached across the table and grabbed the tail of the man's long beard and pulled him down so smartly that his forehead connected with the table sharply, rattling all the used dishes and cutlery left lying there.

'Now that is called an '*expedient solution*', Misty explained. 'So chew on it a while and let me hear my letter, will you?'

The elderly gray beard rubbed his head and frowned, thinking himself lucky he had only finished up in a plate of half finished corn grits, for all knew the capacity of Misty Blue when angered. So he scraped his finger through the remains of the dish and sucked on the leavings contentedly.

'Altercation means dispute,' the innkeeper clarified patiently, him being only too used to the uneducated. He cleared his throat and went on, '*This gentleman, being one Mr. Abernathy Gooding, has proved most unapproachable and although we own*

60

full title and deeds to the property he has taken it upon himself to attempt acts of coercion—'

They all looked expectantly at the gray beard waiting for him to say something. But he had his mouth full at the time so nothing was forthcoming.

'*We are in desperate measures, dear brother, and would ask, that is if you might be so kind, to aid us in this difficult time. Perhaps a persuasive word from you would reassure the gentleman and bring peace once again to our beloved Convent. Your loving sister in Christ, Winifred.'*

Misty sniffed and sat back, all eyes upon him.

'Well,' asked one. 'What you aim to do, Misty?'

Misty rubbed a stubby finger alongside his nose, 'Hardly know the girl.'

'Yes, but she is kin,' urged the innkeeper. 'Surely you will do something.'

'Must be a lot worse than she says,' suggested another. 'Her being a nun and all.'

'Why's that different?' asked Misty.

The man rolled his eyes skywards and folded his hands together as if in prayer, 'You know, them people being all love and charity and such.'

'So?'

'Well, they're mighty forgiving. This Gooding fellow is probably a real asshole and your sister is taking his good side even though it don't sound like he has one.'

Misty thought about it a while and then puffed his cheeks and asked, 'Where is this place?'

'The Convent of Lesser Sorrows,' the innkeeper told him, reading from the letter's heading. 'That will be outside the town of Amesville west of Dillon in the Beaverhead country.'

'Ah, I know it well; leastways it is decent country out there. Dales and rivers amidst the mountains, a fair place indeed.'

'A fair distance as well.'

'Nay, a stroll is all,' boasted Misty who had walked the length of The Rockies from end to end more than once. 'I can do that within a month.'

The Convent of Lesser Sorrows under the evening sunlight was a yellow brick-built structure standing in wooded land and as Misty approached along the driveway he took in the tall central clock tower topped by a cross. On each side of the tower stood lesser tile-roofed abutments with tall curved-topped windows. The entrance itself was of large double doors under an arch of white stone and at the head of the steps awaiting him were two nuns dressed in gray serge tunics with simple coifs covering their heads. Misty approved, it was a pleasant looking place that blended well with its environment.

The smaller of the two women clasped her hands together excitedly, cocked her head to one side and grinned as Misty dismounted his last surviving horse.

'Oh, brother Misty, you came. Oh, bless you brother for coming in our hour of need.'

She was a small diminutive character with pale freckled features and the lightest of blue eyes.

'You Winifred?' asked Misty as he climbed the steps.

'I am, dearest brother. And this is our Mother Superior, Sister Fortitude.'

Misty nodded greeting to the formidable looking Mother Superior, An unmoving and large lady whose expression seemed set in stone. Her tunic did little to alter the appearance of solid granite; the gray scapular she wore was overlaid by a broad leather belt from which dangled a large rosary, the wooden beads the size of small apples.

'Well, Winifred, have to say in all truth, I hardly recognize you 'cept for the freckles. Brother Abner spoke of you when last we met and even then I could barely remember.'

'It was a long time ago, brother. And I was only a child, but how is Abner?'

'Well enough, when last I saw him.'

'You have been told of our troubles, Mr. Blue?' Mother Superior cut in with stern demeanor.

'I have.'

'It is no small matter for us,' she went on, her mouth drawn down as if she were sucking lemons. 'And although I despise all thoughts of aggression and violence we are opposed by the ungodly in this matter and can find no solution but to call on you.'

'We have prayed long and hard,' Winifred promised.

'To no avail,' said Sister Fortitude. 'Still Mr. Gooding persists in his pernicious attacks.' When she said the name it was with a lowered brow and tightly closed eyes as if a cloud had crossed over the sun.

'What 'xactly has this fellow done to cause you such grief?' asked Misty.

'Come, come, we can talk on that later.' fluttered Sister Fortitude suddenly, at last breaking her statue-like pose and ushering Misty inside. 'We are remiss. Sister Winifred, will you tell the sisters to prepare a room and food for Mr. Blue, I'm sure he must be tired and hungry after his journey.'

Misty Blue followed her into the foyer, a thing of mosaic patterned floor and curving cream-colored pillars. As Winifred scampered off, her gray habit flying behind her, Sister Fortitude place a broad hand on Misty's chest to stop him where he stood in the entrance.

'Look here,' she said in a gravelly voice whilst eyeing him sharply. 'I know what manner of man you are, Misty Blue. Have no doubt about it. Afore I came in here to serve the Lord I done all manner of unrighteous things, so I seen something of the world, believe me.' Her voice was deep and little more above a growl. 'These sisters in here are a mixed bag some of them coming to us from bad backgrounds. They been saved all right but they're still all women and they're under my care. You touch any one of them and I'll bust your balls like you wouldn't believe. We clear?'

Misty raised his eyebrows innocently, 'Not my intention and I do believe you,' he said, eyeing the nun's broad shoulders and wide frame.

'I need a man of your caliber and that's the only reason I had Sister Winifred call on you. We follow a Christian teaching here but it don't mean we have to be steamrollered by the likes of Abernathy Gooding. If you can call him off peaceably, all well and good but if you have to smite him then be sure you do it with good force.'

'See what I can do,' promised Misty, a little overcome by this war-like matron.

'Come then and we'll feed you but keep your manners. I'll be watching you,' she warned before briskly turning and walking off. 'And you can leave your weapons here,' she threw over her shoulder.

Misty did as he was told and followed behind, feeling as if he had just entered school for the first time and been admonished by the headmistress.

The dining hall or refectory was a high ceilinged room of large proportions and the nuns gathered there sitting at a long trestle table seemed diminished by the space. Sister Fortitude took her place at the head of the table and she pointed for Misty to occupy the other end. Between them sat the other nuns on either side of the table and Sister Fortitude quickly introduced them all.

'Sister Boniface.' A short, fat and ruby-faced looking creature with flour on her cheek who beamed at Misty with a maternal eye. 'Sister Grace.' A dour looking woman, thin as a rake with her gaze kept downcast and firmly fixed on the table. 'Sister Bendito.' Rather vivacious looking for a nun, with tanned Latin skin, lustrous eyes and full lips whose eager eyes spoke volumes as she cast them over the Mountain Man's bold physique. 'Sister Winifred, you know, of course.' She then addressed the table, 'Sisters, Mister Blue is here to advise us in the matter of Mister Gooding, you shall leave him to do his work without interruption please. Now then, we eat simply here, Mister Blue, I hope it will be to your satisfaction.'

A wooden bowl of boiled oats was placed before Misty and being almighty hungry he dug in immediately and scraped the bowl clean in seconds.

'Ahem!' coughed Sister Fortitude with a single raised eyebrow. 'We usually offer thanksgiving before we begin.'

'Oh! Sorry,' muttered Misty.

The nuns dutifully bowed their heads and muttered Grace before attacking the porridge with slow and purposeful spoons. It seemed to take forever to Misty and when the next dish arrived, a bowl of boiled fish, he took his time and allowed the nuns to take the lead mainly as he had no particular liking for boiled fish.

'You got to tell me. Sister,' said Misty, addressing the Mother Superior. 'Where does this fellow hang out?'

'Mister Gooding occupies a ranch at the foot of the hill,' she replied, altering her earlier rougher tone to one more befitting her situation as head of the Convent. 'Down at the far end of the property that he so wishes to take from us. When not there, I believe his favorite place of residence is a tavern in town called the The Spayed Cat.'

'Might be I should go take me a

drink at this tavern after supper.'

'The Convent door shall be locked and bolted at Compline, so be sure to be back in time.'

'As you say, Sister,' agreed Misty, although he had no idea what a 'Compline' was.

When the meal was over, Misty determined he would need more than a sup of beer at the tavern and set himself to have a good feed as well, for the meal the Sisters enjoyed did little to assuage his appetite. He collected his weapons at the foyer and was about to leave as the Sisters filed off to do something called Vespers, another one that had Misty at a loss. A gray shape flitted after him as he had a hand on the door.

'You will allow me,' said a husky voice, laying a cool slender hand over his on the latch.

Misty turned to see the dark eyes of the Mexican, Sister Bendito upon him.

'Very strong hands you have, señor.'

'It's okay,' said Misty. 'I may be a little slow on the uptake in here but I can still open a door myself.'

'Well,' she breathed. 'If you have need of anything, you will be sure to call on me, won't you?'

The invitation was clear and Misty swallowed as he remembered Sister Fortitude's warning.

''Deed I will,' he said, quickly opening the door and stepping outside.

I t was easy to pick out Gooding in the The Spayed Cat.
He sat separate from the rest at the far end, on a chair slightly higher than the coterie gathered around him. Dressed entirely in white and given

the long white hair that fell to his shoulders and pale skin he had a certain albino look about him. In the dimly lit tavern he stood out like a wart on a whore's nose.

Misty drifted to the bar and ordered, he felt he stood out himself amongst this crowd of cowboys. They all appeared to be hot off the range, dressed in dusty chaps, high-domed hats and flamboyant neckerchiefs. And every one of them had a six-shooter holstered at his waist.

Eyes slowly turned as the cowboys registered that a stranger had entered their domain. The bawdy conversation dropped to a whisper and Misty knew he was the center of attention. He studied the blank wall behind the bar and sipped his drink.

'Don't see many scraggedy-assed trappers in here anymore,' came an overly loud observation from the far end of the bar.

Misty turned to face the crowd and answered loudly, 'That's 'cos us men of the mountains don't often come down low enough to where the worms crawl.'

There was an uneasy muttering at that.

'I'm looking for Abernathy Gooding,' Misty continued. He turned to the figure in white, 'Might that be you, sir?'

Gooding focused down his nose and took a long look at the Mountain Man, 'It is,' he said finally. 'And for what reason do I owe this pleasure?'

Misty set down his glass, 'I come to talk to you about them nuns up there.'

'Indeed,' his accent was lordly but behind it came a slyer version. 'What about them?'

'You say you got claim on their land.'

'Not claim, I own it. They are squatting on my property. Who are you?'

'Name's Misty Blue and I'm here to ask you to lay off them poor women.'

'And what business is it of yours?'

'Let's just say I have a vested interest. Now I start by asking nice but if you want to make it otherwise then I'm at your service. However I must warn you it will not go well for you.'

'Threats!' sneered Gooding. 'Threats from a badly dressed backwoodsman with attitude. I fear I have been too generous to these women, now they hire some dirty roughneck to come threaten me. You hear that, boys? The nuns have a brawny Mountain Man to keep them company. I trust you serve them well, Misty Blue.'

That brought a generous amount of snide laughter from the gathering.

Misty began his chant of accomplishments, which was traditional for the men of the mountains, 'I've walked with the whirlwind, Mister Gooding. Lifted boulders big as houses. Strode across lightning rods and kissed the other side of heaven. Killed me some Cree and fought with the black bear to the death, I've lived off bones and sucked on sticks when the going was hard. Don't bother me if it rains for a year or the sun shines for a century, it's all the same to me. I'm a man of the mountains where the air is clean and I can smell you from here for the feral rat you are.'

'Oh, dear,' Gooding hiccupped a laugh. 'What a colorful fellow, and where did you first appear on stage, may I ask?'

'I'm a man of my word, sir. And I tell you this, leave those religious alone or suffer my wrath.'

Gooding's face dropped, 'I think our friend needs to leave. Perhaps some of you might help him on his way.'

The brawl that followed was a bloody affair with Misty snapping a few arms as if they were kindling, kicking a few crotches, extracting a few teeth, boxing a few ears and generally acquitting himself quite well. That was until one brawny fellow with a very large head and shoulders to match brought down a bar stool on Misty's head and sent him into dreamland.

He awoke to find it was full dark and that he was bound ankle and foot and balanced on a pine-pole gate. The rope around his neck was tethered to an overhead post that bore the title 'Gooding Ranch' on a sign drawn in poker burnt letters.

The crowd of cowboys was gathered around his feet and Gooding sat watching from the back of a magnificent white horse.

'I believe Mister Blue is with us again,' said Gooding. 'You may release him to his own balance now.'

The hands that held Misty aloft instantly let go and Misty wavered as he struggled to keep himself upright on the narrow pole with the soles of his moccasin boots.

'Yes, it could be a long night for you, Mountain Man,' sneered Gooding. 'Eventually you will tire and then it will be a long goodnight forever, I fear.'

'You're looking at your own coffin when you look on me, Gooding,' Misty replied calmly.

The rancher chuckled deep in his chest, 'Oh, yes, of a certain. All I have to do is fear a man tied up like a monkey on a stick with a noose around his neck, I quiver with anticipation. Come now boys, let's leave Mister Blue to his nightly considerations, we have work to do tomorrow and must be about early.'

Gooding turned his horse away and the men followed on behind. The rancher twisted in the saddle for one last word, 'I have had enough of these wretched women; come the morning I intend to burn the God-loving bitches out. Perhaps you will meet up with them in that heaven they promise, although I suspect your destination will be a far warmer place.'

When he was alone, Misty teetered on the pole and tried to look around for some means of escape. Every twitch was a movement closer to his feet sliding and strangling himself. But with the adroitness of a mountain goat he managed to tightrope walk

and shuffled along to one side of the gate. There he rested, leaning his back against the post for support. It took off some of the strain from the rough noose around his neck and gave Misty time to consider. The post he leaned against was rough and not bark-stripped and he determined to attempt losing the bonds at his wrists with a rapid up and down motion, the friction eventually burning through the rope. Still not an easy thing to do when you're balanced like a ballerina in a circus show.

It took him an hour and a half but finally the rope parted and his hands were free to remove the noose. It was a simple thing after that to jump down and free his legs and Misty then eased his aching shoulders and planned his next move.

The ranch house was in sight; Misty could see the bunkhouse and main building in the moonlight from where he crouched.

It was getting near dawn by the time Misty had worked his silent way in close to the building. He came by the corral and noted the twenty or so ponies they had in there. With care he slid open the gate and quietly chased the ponies free, then he moved across to a storage shed beside the barn. His weapons were gone, taken whilst he was unconscious, and he was in dire need of something to defend himself.

Amongst the racks of tools he found a long handled pitchfork, and a ball peen hammer but considering the pitchfork too long he cracked the wood across his knee until he had a hand weapon with five sharp prongs. The hammer he slid into his belt to take the place of his tomahawk. He was about to move on when he noticed metal cans stacked off to one corner. Coal oil for the lamps.

'We'll see who burns who out,' Misty muttered to himself.

Moving like a ghost amongst the shadows Misty lay a trail, circling the main house with an open topped can that sloshed a steady river of the inflammable liquid. After emptying five cans in this way his sensitive nostrils picked up the scent of cigar smoke coming from the direction of the bunkhouse and he moved in that direction.

Leaning against the hitching rail a lone nighthawk was taking his first smoke of the day before riding out on watch. In the moonlight his outline was perfect as Misty slid silently up behind him.

'You got a light?' Misty whispered in the man's ear. His own tinderbox had been taken along with his satchel so he had a need.

'Sure thing,' said the unsuspecting fellow just before Misty spitted him on the pitchfork. The cowboy said no more as his tongue was pinned to the roof of his mouth by the steel tines that ran right through his jaw and on into the base of the brain. As the fellow dropped, Misty reached out and lifted the burning cigar from his nerveless fingers.

'Obliged,' he said, blowing on the glowing coal.

With a long underhand toss Misty threw the cigar butt in a sparking curve that landed in the swamp of coal oil lying around the ranch building. With a great 'boof!' of sound the fire started and ran in a fast stream to encircle the ranch house.

Misty dragged the dead man out of sight and slid the cowboy's pistol from his holster; he checked the action and saw it was fully loaded. He cocked the gun and let loose a shot into the air, frightening the remaining ponies in the corral into panicked flight.

There was a rumble of sound from inside the bunkhouse.

'What the hell's that?'

'Something's up.'

'Well, go see.'

'Dang it! I ain't got no clothes on, you go.'

Misty slid back into the shadows as the bunkhouse door swung open.

'The ponies are out!' yelled a voice.

More clumping feet and then, 'Goddamn! Look here, the main house is on fire.'

'Get the water.'

'No, get the ponies. I got me two hundred buck's worth of prime horseflesh out there. Trained it up from a colt.'

'What about Gooding?'

'He ain't worth no two-hundred bucks, come on!'

The cowboys tumbled out into the darkness and made off at the run after their steeds. As Misty had surmised the animals were their main source of income and far more precious to them than their boss.

Misty waited patiently for Gooding to make a show.

Ringed by five-foot high flames, he finally made it to his front door. 'Fire!' he yelled. 'We're on fire!' He stood on his front porch clothed in a long white nightshirt with the surrounding mote of flames making it impossible to escape. The brutal light flickered over his whiteness, from the long hair and pale skin down to the thin bare legs showing at the bottom of the shirt.

Misty strode up and stood on the opposite side of the blaze and waited for the rancher to see him.

'*You!*' spat Gooding. 'Go get some water before the whole place goes up.'

'Don't say I didn't warn you,' Misty answered.

'Damn you!' spat Gooding. He reached inside the door and pulled out a Springfield rifle, levering back the hammer as he did so. 'Get me out of this or I'll blast you,' he ordered.

'That my gun?' Misty asked quizzically.

'Doesn't matter where the bullet comes from, does it? You'll be dead just the same, now do as I say.'

'I think your nightshirt's smoldering,' Misty observed.

Automatically, Gooding looked down and as he glanced away Misty slid the ball peen hammer from his belt.

Snarling in anger, Gooding returned his attention to Misty and leveled the rifle. He fired but Misty was already on the move, ducking behind the cover of the raging fire.

One side of the building was already alight, the dry wooden boards only waiting fuel for the hungry blaze.

'You're going to fry, Gooding,' called Misty, popping up from a different position as the rancher fumbled with his reload.

Gooding swiveled around, the intense heat bringing sweat to his brow. Suddenly, he saw the flames part, a rapid tunnel of free air made a black hole in the wall of fire. Something came at him, turning end over end in its whispering flight from out of the darkness.

When the hammer struck it buried itself a good inch into Gooding's skull. He dropped the rifle and sat down with legs spread wide, propped up by the wall behind. His eyes stared out of his cracked head the body unable to do more.

Misty watched as the porch above Gooding caught alight, the bark shingle crackling under the racing flames. He stood there until the raging porch collapsed over the sitting figure and the flames made their steady way inside the house. When the whole place was a boiling pillar of flame, only then did Misty turn his back and walk away into the night.

When Misty hammered on the Convent door, dawn light was breaking through the trees along the driveway.

'Be silent,' hissed Sister Bendito. 'The Sisters are at Matins, your noise will disturb their prayers.'

'Sorry about that,' apologized Misty. 'Bit early for beating the mats though?'

'And where have you been all night? You smell of smoke.'

'It was cold out, I made a little fire.'

'You have not slept? You must be very tired.'

'Amen to that,' yawned Misty.

'Then come,' smiled the frisky Sister Bendito, arching a seductive eyebrow. 'I will turn down your bed for you.'

And that ain't all, I wager, surmised the Mountain Man, although, he reasoned, tired as he was he was in no mood to turn down anything.

THE MARSHALL GROVER STORY

DAVID WHITEHEAD REMEMBERS A TRUE LEGEND

Few writers are fortunate enough to number their books in the hundreds, but Leonard F Meares was one of them. When he died in 1993, Len could lay claim to more than 700 published novels—746, to be precise—the overwhelming majority of which were westerns.

Leonard Frank Meares was best known to western fans the world over as "Marshall Grover", creator of Texas trouble-shooters Larry and Stretch. He was born in Sydney, Australia, on 13 February 1921, and started reading the westerns of Zane Grey, Clarence E Mulford and William Colt MacDonald when he was still a child. A lifelong movie buff with a particular fondness for shoot-'em-ups, he later recalled, "At that early age I got a kick out of the humorous patches often seen in Buck Jones films, and realized that humor should always be an integral part of any western."

Len worked at a variety of jobs after leaving school, including shoe salesman, and during the Second World War he served with the Royal Australian Air Force. When he returned to civilian life in 1946, he went to work at Australia's Department of Immigration.

The aspiring author bought his first typewriter in the mid-1950s with the intention of writing for radio and cinema, but when this proved to be easier said than done, he decided to try his hand at popular fiction instead. Since a great many paperback westerns were being published locally, he set about writing one of his own. The result, *Trouble Town*, was published by the Cleveland Publishing Company in 1955. Although Len had devised the pseudonym "Marshall Grover" for his first book, however, Cleveland decided to issue it under the name Johnny Nelson. "I'm still chagrined about that!" he told me years later. Undaunted, he quickly developed a facility for writing westerns, and Cleveland eventually put him under contract.

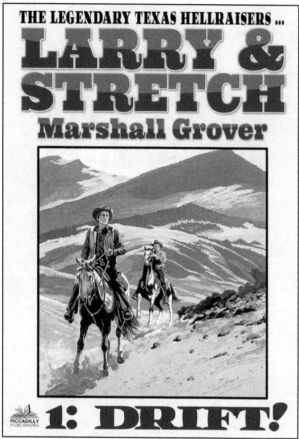

THE LEGENDARY TEXAS HELLRAISERS ...

LARRY & STRETCH

Marshall Grover

1: DRIFT!

His tenth yarn, *Drift!*, (1956), introduced his fiddle-footed knights-errant, Larry Valentine and Stretch Emerson, the characters for which he would eventually become so beloved. And nowhere was the author's quirky sense of humor more apparent than in these action-packed and always painstakingly plotted yarns.

With his work appearing under such names as "Ward Brennan", "Glenn Murrell", "Shad Denver" and even "Brett Waring" (a pseudonym more correctly associated with Keith Hetherington), Len never needed more than 24 hours to devise a new plot. "Irving Berlin once said that there are so many notes on a keyboard from which to create a new melody, and it's the same with writing on a treadmill basis."

At his most prolific, the by-now full-time writer could turn out around thirty books a year. In 1960, he created a brief but memorable series of westerns set in and around the town of Bleak Creek. Four years later came *The Night McLennan Died*, the first of more than 70 oaters to feature cavalryman-turned-manhunter Big Jim Rand.

In mid-1966, Len left Cleveland and started writing exclusively for the Horwitz Group. Quick to exploit its latest asset, Horwitz soon sold more than 30 novels to Bantam Books for publication in the United States, where for legal reasons "Marshall Grover" became "Marshall McCoy", "Larry and Stretch" became "Larry and Streak" and "Big Jim" became "Nevada Jim Gage". With their tighter editing and wonderful James Bama covers, I believe the westerns issued during this period are probably the author's best.

Although I started reading the Larry and Stretch series when I was about 10 years old, it wasn't until 1979 (and I had reached the ripe old age of 21) that I finally decided to contact the author, via his publisher. When he eventually replied, I discovered a genial, self-deprecating and incredibly genuine man who showed real interest in his readers. And

a new Marshall Grover western

BLEAK CREEK

No. 765
CLEVELAND
2/- AUST

since we seemed to hit it off so well, what started out as a simple, one-off letter of appreciation quickly blossomed into a warm and lively correspondence which was to last for 14

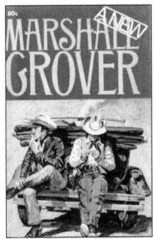

years.

Len began his association with Robert Hale Limited in 1981, with *Jo Jo and the Private Eye*, the first of five "Marty Moon" detective novels published under the name "Lester

Malloy". Hale also issued his offbeat romance, *The Future and Philomena*, as by "Val Sterling", in 1982. He even scored with two stand-alone crime novels, *The Battle of Jericho Street* (1984) as by "Frank Everton", and *Dead Man Smiling* (1986), published under his own name.

His first Black Horse Western was, fittingly enough, a Larry and Stretch yarn entitled *Rescue a Tall Texan* (1989). It's an entertaining entry in the long-running series in which Stretch, the homely, amiable but always slower-witted half of the duo, is kidnapped by an outlaw gang in need of a hostage. Naturally, Larry quickly sets out to track down and rescue his partner, and is joined along the way by an erudite half-Sioux Indian with the unlikely name of Cathcart P. Slow Wolf, and the always-apoplectic Pinkerton operative, Dan Hoolihan, both popular recurring characters in the series. The climax is a typically robust shootout in which Larry and Stretch mix it up with no less than 13 hardcases—13, in this instance, proving to be an extremely unlucky number for the bad guys.

Len also decided to create a new double-act specifically for the Black Horse Western market, in the shape of husband-and-wife detectives Rick and Hattie Braddock.

Rick and Hattie first appeared in *Colorado Runaround*, published in 1991. Rick is a former cowboy, actor and gambler, Hattie (nee Keever) a one-time magician's assistant, chorus girl and knife-thrower's target. Thrown together by circumstances, the couple eventually fall in love, get spliced and set up the Braddock Detective Agency. Their first case involves the disappearance of a wealthy rancher's daughter, and it takes place—as did all of Len's westerns—on an historically sketchy but always largely good-natured frontier, where the harsh realities of life seldom make an appearance.

And in that last respect, Len's fiction always reflected his own character, for here was a very moral and fair-minded man with a commendably innocent, straightforward and

almost naive outlook on life—a man who would always rather see the good in a person, place or situation than the bad.

Colorado Runaround, like the BHWs which followed it, is typical—though not vintage—Meares. There's a deceptively intricate plot, regular bursts of action, oddball supporting characters and plenty of laughs. In all respects, it is the work of a writer's writer. But the humor is somewhat hit-or-miss, and is as likely to make the story as break it.

This observation also applies to Len's three "Rick and Hattie" sequels, *The Major and the Miners* (1992), in which the heroes attempt to solve a whole passel of mysteries and restore peace to an increasingly restive mining town; *Five Deadly Shadows* (1993), a far more satisfying kidnap story; and *Feud at Greco Canyon* (1994), in which the happily married sleuths work overtime to avert a full-scale range-war.

Len's final western series, set in Rampart County, Montana, is probably his most disappointing. *Montana Crisis* (1993) is a pretty standard tale about how a growing town gets a sheriff—in the form of overly officious ex-Pinkerton operative Francis X. Rooney—and his laconic deputy, Memphis Beck. In the first adventure, they break the iron rule of megalomaniac entrepreneur Leon Coghill, but curiously, there's more talk than action.

Things perk up a bit in the sequel, *Rooney's Second Deputy* (1994), a mystery that also involves a daring robbery.

Thus, it's probably fairer to judge Len's undoubted merits as a western writer more on his Cleveland and Horwitz titles—which I cannot praise highly enough—than those he wrote for Hale. But why should this be?

To answer that question, we need to understand what was happening in Len's professional life at that time they were written.

In the spring of 1991, the author was requested by Horwitz not to produce any more Larry and Stretch westerns for six months. Apparently, Horwitz had built up a substantial backlog of material, and couldn't see much point in buying new manuscripts when there were so many older ones still awaiting publication. It was during this period that Len wrote and sold his first BHW.

When he delivered his next "Marshall Grover" book ahead of Christmas 1991, however, Horwitz dropped a bombshell. The company had decided to close down its paperback arm altogether, and in future would only require one Larry and Stretch story each month (as against the two Len usually produced), to sell on to the still-buoyant Scandinavian market.

Len's wife, Vida, put it this way: "He was more or less sacked."

Len's immediate instinct was to find another publisher and continue writing Marshall Grover westerns for the English-speaking market. Under the terms of his contract, however, Horwitz owned both the Grover name and the Grover characters—and weren't about to allow him to take them anywhere else.

To a man who had spent 36 years as "the Marshall", and almost as long writing literally hundreds of Larry and Stretch yarns, it was a devastating turn of events—not least financially—and Len quickly went into decline. In a letter to me, Vida Meares remembered, "When out of our home or talking on the phone, [Len] was still the same cheerful, quick-witted man, but at home he was down-hearted and feeling well-nigh finished."

And though he continued to write Larry and Stretch, he often told me how unhappy he was that his English-speaking fans, who had stuck with the series for so long, would no longer get the chance to follow the Texans' adventures.

This, then, was the backdrop against which Len wrote his Black Horse Westerns. In low spirits, and with his professional life in turmoil, I believe he was attempting to create new characters to replace those who had become his constant companions over the years, and whom he viewed very much as his "children". But though he gave each and every one of his BHWs as much care and attention as possible, Larry and Stretch proved to be an impossible act to follow—which only depressed him more.

Just over a year later, in January 1993, Len contracted viral pneumonia and was hospitalized for the condition. His daughter Gaby later wrote to me, "When I visited him on 3 February, he was giving the nurses cheek and, as usual, more concerned about my mother's welfare than his own." Early the following morning, however, he took a sudden turn for the worse and passed away in his sleep.

Vida Meares told me, "Marshall Grover and my husband were the same person—and Horwitz killed Marshall Grover."

Though this was clearly not the case, I do believe that the decision taken by Horwitz to stop publishing Larry and Stretch, coupled with their refusal to allow him to take his pseudonym and characters elsewhere, certainly contributed to Len's decline.

The last two Leonard Meares books to appear in the BHW line—*Tin Star Trio* (1994) and *A Quest of Heroes* (1996)—were written not by Len at all, but by Link Hullar (himself the author of five BHWs) and myself, from fragments found among Len's papers.

Tin Star Trio began life as an untitled short story featuring two drifters called Zack Holley and Curly Ryker. As soon as I started reading it, I realized that Len had been toying with the idea of continuing to write Larry and Stretch—most probably for publication by Hale—but changing the characters' names to avoid any legal difficulties. The story revolved around a missing cashbox hidden in a remote canyon, and told how Zack and Curly manage to thwart the attempts of a band of outlaws to retrieve it.

Link and I both felt that it would be a nice to expand the story into a short novel, and with the blessing of Vida Meares, that's exactly what we did. Although we aged the characters a little (because we've both always preferred westerns that feature older, slightly over-the-hill heroes), we tried to recapture some of the spirit of Len at his best. Even the titles of the chapters are all taken from previous Larry and Stretch books.

A Quest of Heroes came about at the suggestion of Australian singer Dave Mathewson, a Marshall Grover fan from way back, who had earlier recorded a sort of "tribute album" entitled *The Marshall, Larry and Stretch and Me and You*. Dave's brief plot, which was all about a bandit gang who kidnap white women in order to sell them into slavery south of the border, gave us an ideal opportunity to bring back not just Larry and Stretch (here once again masquerading as Zack and Curly), but all of Len's best-known characters, including Big Jim Rand, Slow Wolf, Dan Hoolihan and more. Naturally, we had to change the names of all the main players, but I like to think that we produced a book that Len would have approved of.

In his own books, you can find Len himself was in every line, and re-reading them is like visiting with him again. He was a skilled and tireless writer, a truly wonderful friend, and I remember him—will *always* remember him—with tremendous affection.

J. T. EDSON

DRAW POKER'S SUCH A SIMPLE GAME

Despite the large number of people on the sidewalks of a busy street in the business section of Topeka, or rather due to his desire to impress them, and two attractive female passengers with his skill, the young and newly appointed driver of the Wells Fargo stagecoach was keeping his six-horse team moving at a far greater speed than was wise for such a well populated area. However, it could not be said that he was entirely to blame for what happened next. Having watched him approaching with a fixed intensity, the well dressed young woman with a pretty face which was pale and distraught in its expression suddenly stepped into the street and started across it not too far ahead.

Letting out a startled exclamation, the driver responded to the danger with an admirable presence of mind. Applying the brake with his right boot, he let his whip slip between his legs. Then he braced both feet against the front of the driving box and, thrusting his body backwards, pulled with both hands on the reins in an attempt to either halt or turn the horses aside before they reached the young woman. Although the shotgun messenger at his side gave an unnecessary bellow of warning and grabbed for the leather ribbons to help, it was obvious even their combined efforts could not bring the powerful animals and fast moving vehicle to a stop in time to prevent an accident. In fact, it appeared nothing could save the young woman from her apparently imprudent and ill-advised actions.

Although masculine shouts and feminine screams arose from all sides, the person to respond most quickly to the situation was, despite her attire suggesting otherwise, most certainly *not* a man!

Five foot seven in height, in her late 'teens, the fastest to think and act had a battered dark blue U.S. Cavalry *kepi* perched at a rakish angle on her head. Her shortish and curly mop of fiery red hair framed a face which was tanned, freckled, pretty and generally merry looking. Rising firmly round and full, her breasts forced against the material of a well worn, but clean, fringed buckskin shirt which was open low enough at the neck to present a tantalizing glimpse of the valley between the mounds. Trimming at the waist, obviously without any artificial aids, her torso expanded to form curvaceous hips fitting snugly into buckskin pants and set upon sturdily eye-catching legs. She had Pawnee moccasins on her feet and having the sleeves of the shirt rolled up above the elbows exposed arms more muscular than a lady of fashion would have cared for. Not that anybody would have suspected her of being one. Although her attire indicat-

Art by Julien Vandois

ed she came from further west where such items were common, because of a ban imposed by the city's authorities, she did not have on a gun-belt and holstered revolver. However, the handle of a coiled, long-lashed bull whip was thrust through the leather loop attached at the left of the broad brown belt around her waist.

Hurtling from the raised sidewalk, the redhead alighted running like a sprinter in a race over a much more level surface than the hard and wheel-rutted street. While she was achieving a most creditable speed, it would clearly be a very close thing whether she would achieve her purpose, or join the young woman as a victim of the rapidly approaching horses and stagecoach. Throwing herself through the air for the last few feet, after the fashion of a player performing a tackle in a 'Boston game', she wrapped her arms around the slender waist of the woman. The impetus of her arrival carried them both onwards to safety, but with such a close margin that the wheels of the vehicle passed behind them by not more than a couple of inches.

Keeping going, unaware of just how narrow an escape they had had, the rescuer and the rescued were unable to retain their equilibrium and they sprawled to the ground at the feet of another person of their sex who had reacted with commendable promptitude, albeit an instant too late to be of assistance.

About an inch taller than the redhead, of indeterminate age, the second would-be rescuer wore the black and white habit of a nun. Although such an item was not usual for her kind, she had on thin black leather gloves. Not unexpectedly, other than suggesting her figure might be more bulky than curvaceous, the conventional garments of her vocation prevented any indication of its contours from being revealed. Whatever good looks nature might have endowed upon her were marred by a pair of large, horn-rimmed spectacles and sallow features with a somewhat bulbous nose above prominent 'rabbit' teeth.

Although the nun had quit the opposite sidewalk with surprising speed for one of her appearance, she had come to a halt when she saw the girl would reach the young woman before she could. However, as they sprawled in a tangle together at her feet, she bent over them in a solicitous manner. Reaching out with both hands, she hooked them under the armpits of the buckskin shirt and lifted the redhead erect.

If the ease with which the girl found

herself elevated came as a surprise to her, what happened next was even more so!

'I'm real pleased you did that, Calam!' the nun whispered into the redhead's ear, her accent being indicative of a well educated upbringing somewhere south of the Mason-Dixon line. 'It would have drawn more attention my way than I need right now if I'd had to.'

'Thanks, sister,' the girl said, as she was released by the woman in the habit of a nun, but whose words had indicated the attire was misleading.

Amongst her other talents, Martha "Calamity Jane" Canary could justifiably consider herself an excellent poker player. In fact, she often claimed that nothing could surprise her. Nevertheless, she needed all the skill she had developed at controlling her emotions to avoid showing surprise over the words and the realization that the 'nun' was none other than the lady outlaw, Belle Starr. Looking around quickly into the less than attractive face, she knew she would never have made the identification without receiving the evidence of the voice. Taking notice of what had been said, and drawing the required conclusion, even though she could not see any peace officers among the people who were gathering around, she refrained from saying anything which might inform them of the true state of affairs.

However, the response from the young woman who had been saved was hardly what might have been expected!

'Wh-why did you have to *interfere*!' Ruby Wakefield asked in anguished tones which established her background was the mid-West and of affluent circumstances.

'It seemed like a good thing to do,' Calamity answered coldly, puzzled by such an attitude on the part of a person she had rescued from serious injury, if not death, at some considerable risk to her own well being.

'I-I'm sorry,' the young woman replied with genuine contrition, looking from the redhead to Belle Starr and back. 'But I didn't want sav—!'

'Don't say any more, my child,' the lady outlaw instructed, in a different tone to that used when addressing the redhead. It had, in fact, lost its Southern drawl and taken on a timbre suggestive of Irish origins and with a note of authority such as a certain kind of nun would employ. 'You don't want *strangers* to know what you were *trying* to do. Now do you?'

'No-*NO*!' Ruby admitted, a full realization of the enormity of her behavior striking her and, twisting into Belle's arms to bury her face against the black habit, she burst into tears.

'There, there!' the lady outlaw soothed, wondering what turn of events could have caused the well dressed and respectable looking young woman to attempt suicide, particularly in such a public and potentially messy fashion. 'I think you had better come with me to somewhere we can talk.'

'B-But I'm n-not a Ca-Catholic,' Ruby objected, looking up.

'And neither am I,' Belle replied, which was true enough even though the rest of her statement was not. 'I belong to a Protestant order. Come along.'

'All right, folks,' Calamity said, swinging around and looking in a prohibitive fashion at the people who were moving forward and talking excitedly amongst themselves. 'It's all over 'n' done with, so let's leave it that way.'

'Is she all right?' a man inquired.

'Sure,' the redhead replied, then glanced along the street.

Having brought the stagecoach to a halt, Michael Gilhooley was springing down from his seat on the right side of the driving box. The expression on his face indicated he was both shaken and infuriated by the narrowly avoided accident. After having made the sign of the cross, grasping his long-handled, long-lashed whip in his right fist, he stalked forward with his face suffused by rage. Seeing him coming and taking note of his demeanor, even those onlookers who did not know how uncertain his temper became when he was aroused read the signs and parted to let him through.

'And just what the *hell* kind of game is it you reckon you were playing?' the driver bellowed furiously in a broad Irish brogue, catching Ruby by the shoulder and pulling her away from Belle.

'Take it *easy,* feller!' Calamity snapped, before the young woman she had saved could reply.

'And who the hell was it asking *you* to be pushing your nose in?' Gilhooley demanded. Releasing Ruby, who twisted back into Belle's arms, he swung around to raise the whip in a menacing gesture. Having caught only a fleeting glimpse of the redhead while the rescue was taking place, he had noticed her masculine attire and was now too enraged to give the slightest consideration to her gender, 'Mind you own affairs, or it's getting busted it'll be!'

Which, as anybody who knew Calamity could have warned, was not the kind of attitude to take with her at the best of times. While generally good natured, generous to a fault and possessed of a lively sense of humor, it was not her way—particularly when considering she was in the right—to let herself be put upon or abused. What is more, having come through a dangerous and trying situation, she was even less inclined to accept the words and threatening behavior from the person in part responsible for it. Jumping away from Belle and Ruby, she halted nearer the center of the street and with a clear space around her in which to take action should it prove necessary. Bringing the bull whip from its belt loop swiftly, she caused its long lash to uncoil behind her with the deft ease which told of much practice.

'You just *try* busting my nose!' the redhead declared, standing with feet spread apart and moving her right hand in a way which caused the length of plaited leather to writhe almost as if it possessed a life of its own. 'And my lil friend here'll have *plenty* to say about it!'

'So that's the way of it, huh!' Gilhooley growled, as he ran his gaze over the girl from top to toe, an appreciation of the true state of affairs beginning to assail him. Returning his eyes to studying the twin mounds of what were most definitely *not* masculine flesh forced against the neckline of the buckskin shirt, he went on in a puzzled—but only slightly less hostile—tone, 'Hey, you're not a *man*!'

'My momma told me *that* when I was knee high to a frog,' the redhead answered, watching the different—yet equally dangerous—type of whip in the driver's hand, and ready to counter any move it made in her direction. 'Top of which, 'bout the same time, she telled me *never* to run a six-hoss team 'n' wagon lickety-split through a town where folks was walking about.'

'Well now,' the driver growled, hearing a rumble of concurrence with the comment coming from the people around and realizing that his attempt at an impressive arrival had been ruined. The thought did nothing to improve his temper. Therefore, although he refrained from any kind of aggressive action, his Irish temperament would not allow him to let it be imagined he had been deterred by a mere woman. 'You're one of *them* as the town's got so many of right now, are you?'

'One of which *them*?' Calamity inquired, having only arrived an hour earlier and knowing nothing more about Topeka's current affairs than that it was in the throes of an election of some kind.

'Them "Votes For *Women*" bunch's are running 'round making goddamned nuisances of themselves,' Gilhooley explained, his tone showing his antipathy to members of the opposite sex who behaved in such a fashion. 'Sure and you *look* like you could be. All dressed up like a man and it's thinking you are that you can be acting like one.'

Watching and listening, Belle did not care for the way in which the situation was developing. Having glanced around while first comforting the young woman, she had drawn some satisfaction from there not being any peace officers on the scene. However, some would quickly put in an appearance if there should be trouble and she had no desire to be questioned by them about her involvement in the incident. With that in mind, she wanted to try to prevent hostilities taking place, and the extensive knowledge of human nature she had acquired as an adjunct to her illicit activities, which mostly involved various types of confidence tricks, offered a possible solution. She too had seen the driver make the sign of the cross and considered, when used in conjunction with the way she was dressed, this offered the means by which she could try and achieve her purpose.

'Just a moment, my son,' Belle put in, gently freeing herself from Ruby and walking between Gilhooley and the redhead before the latter would deliver what she knew would be a blistering response calculated to make the situation worse. Noticing the change which came to the driver's face as he ran his gaze over her attire, she concluded her gamble had a chance of paying off. 'There is no reason *whatsoever* for hard words, or threats to this young woman. It was *my* fault the young *lady* started across the street without watching where she was going and needed to be saved.'

'Was that the way of it, sister?' Gilhooley inquired, losing his attitude of aggression and allowing the whip to sink until dangling at his side.

'*Mother Superior,*' the lady outlaw corrected with a cold haughtiness which suggested she considered the term, 'sister', *infra dig* when addressed to one of a much higher status. Knowing how great an authority members of the Catholic church could exercise over people of their faith, she adopted the tone and attitude to give her disguise an even greater potency. 'She's a novice for our Order and, *naturally* was hurrying to meet me.'

'Sure and I'm *sorry,* Mother Superior,' Gilhooley apologized. Memories of the dominance exerted by women in similar positions of authority when he was a child acting as a strong inducement to subservience despite the superiority he always claimed over other members of her sex. 'I wasn't knowing that.'

'Then perhaps you should be *willing* to let bygones be bygones?' Belle hinted, although her tone and demeanor implied the words were more in the nature of a command. Receiving a hurried nod of concurrence from the driver and noticing with approval that Calamity was coiling and returning the whip to its belt loop—a gesture which she saw he had also observed and which was causing him to relax still more—she went on, 'Bless you, my son. Now why don't you take your stagecoach to the depot where I'm sure they're waiting for it, and the pas-

sengers will be wanting to praise you for the skilful way you avoided an accident.'

'I'll be doing just that,' Gilhooley agreed and turned to walk away.

'And now, young lady,' Belle said, as she and the redhead returned to where Ruby was standing. 'I think you had better come along with us—!'

'But you told me that you're a *Protestant,*' the young woman protested, her religious upbringing having installed a mistrust of everything to do with the Catholic faith and overriding a natural desire to do as she was instructed.

'I didn't say I was any different to anybody else, now did I?' the lady outlaw inquired with a smile. Glancing around, she discovered, as she had expected, the crowd had decided there would be no more dramatic or interesting developments and had started to go about their respective businesses. Still consumed by curiosity and wanting to try and prevent a further attempt at suicide, using some other method, she went on in a more commanding tone, 'Come along.'

'I've got some things to do right now, *Mother Superior,*' Calamity remarked. 'But I'd admire to see you later.'

'Very well, my child,' Belle assented. 'I'm staying at Mrs. Lane's Boarding House, if you know where it is.'

'I reckon I can find it,' the redhead declared, filled with admiration for the way in which the lady outlaw was playing the latest character she had created and sharing the interest in why the young woman had behaved in such a way. 'I'll be there in an hour or so.'

* * *

'I really admired the way you stood

up to that *man.'*

Hearing a female voice with the accent of a well educated Bostonian coming from her rear as she was strolling along the sidewalk, Calamity Jane decided the words were meant for her. Glancing over her shoulder, although there were other people looking at her with curiosity and interest, she had no difficulty in deciding who had spoken. About her height, slender to the point of being bony and perhaps ten years older, the woman coming towards the redhead had plain features which were not given even the moderate amount of makeup acceptable for one classed 'good' by the standards of the day anywhere west of the Mississippi River. She had what could have been a man's flat cap on mousey-brown hair taken back tightly into a bun for an effect as unflattering as the rest of her attire. Of excellent quality, there was a masculine cut about her black two-piece travelling outfit and her plain white blouse was adorned by a man's tie.

'Shucks,' Calamity replied, hesitating for a couple of seconds before accepting the right hand thrust towards her. Feeling it tighten on her own, she could not resist the temptation to squeeze back and, on seeing a look of pain mingled with some other emotion she could not decipher, she released her hold. 'Us drivers allus cut loose a mite when we're het up.'

'Are you the *driver* of a stagecoach?' the woman asked with open admiration, retaining her hold until the redhead's hand was drawn free,

'Hell, *no!*' Calamity denied, and pride in her occupation caused her to make an explanation even though she felt vaguely uneasy in the other's presence. 'I did *once,* not that I'd want it *known,* 'cause I handle a Conestoga freight wagon for Dobe Killem full-time and I've got to get going and see about 'tending to it.'

'That is *marvelous!*' the woman enthused, falling into step alongside the redhead. 'Becoming a *driver,* I mean.'

'It's just a chore,' Calamity claimed off-handedly, feeling puzzled by her not particularly welcome companion's attitude and obvious desire for her company. The majority of 'good' women with whom she came into contact, especially those from the east, disapproved of her way of life and adoption of masculine clothing. 'And it sure beats 'n' pays a whole heap better'n anything else I could be doing.'

'That's *very* true,' the woman declared, putting a hand on the redhead's bicep and squeezing gently as if to test its size and firmness. 'There are *so few* kinds of employment men leave open to *us.* By the way, I'm Linda Bell.'

'Howdy,' the girl said, but ignored the right hand thrust her way. Wondering if the interest was caused by the highly colored stories about her which she had heard were circulating in the East, she was disinclined to supply her sobriquet in case it increased the eagerness for her company. 'The name's Martha Jane Canary.'

'Call me "Bell",' the woman requested, pouting a little over the refusal to respond to her gesture. 'Do the *men* object to you being a driver, *Canary?*'

'Only happen I run a wheel over their foot,' Calamity answered, deciding she disliked her surname even more now she had heard it expressed in such a fashion.

'Do you *often*—?' the woman began in what seemed to be a hopeful tone. Then she went on in a tone of disapproval. 'Oh, you're only j*oking!*'

'I'd hate like hell not to be,' Calamity replied and, in the hope of being able to part company with her unwelcome companion, gestured to an alley they were passing. 'Well, I have to go down *this* way.'

'I hope I can meet you *again,* Canary,' Bell declared, following the redhead into the gap between the buildings and once more putting a hand on her sleeve. 'In fact, I'm sure you would enjoy the group I'm in town with for the election. We're the "Women's Rights Movement" and and it's our purpose to ensure women have *complete* equality with men in *everything.* The others would be delighted to meet you and have you address them on your experiences.'

'Well now,' Calamity said, considering there was nothing she wanted less than to meet with such a group. While of a sturdy and independent nature which made her willing and able to meet men on their own terms in many ways, she was far from being a rampant feminist and, in fact, had never even heard the term. Therefore, she was quite content to accept there were several things they could do which were beyond the abilities of any member of her gender. What was more, from what she had seen of others of her sex expressing a similar point of view to that of Linda Bell, she considered they did more harm than good for the rest-of Womankind with their attitudes and behavior. 'I'm not much of a talker.'

'We don't just *talk,* my dear,' Bell said in a conspiratorial fashion, moving around until confronting the redhead and placing both hands on her arms. 'In fact, we have quite a lot of *fun* together.'

With a sensation like being struck by an icy deluge, the realization of what was implied by Bell's last sentence came to Calamity. Because of the circumstances in which she had grown up, her conventional education was lacking and, in any case, such things were not included on the curriculum of schools in those days. However, she was far from being naive and unworldly. While she had never encountered such a person until that moment, from what she had heard said by the rest of Cecil 'Dobey' Killem's drivers and other acquaintances of both sexes—none of whom had such inclinations and all of whom considered those who had to be most undesirable company—she was aware that homosexuality existed and was not purely the province of the male gender. Although far from being a prude, like any normal person on finding herself faced by it for the first time, she felt a flood of revulsion.

'So I'll tell the rest of the group you'll come,' Bell continued, before any reply could be made. Running her arms over the sleeves of Calamity's buckskin shirt, that and the rest of the masculine attire made her feel sure the redhead must wear such clothing to flaunt a disdain for convention, and also shared her sexual proclivities. She thrust her face closer, 'I have to get back now myself, but I'll come and fetch you tonight if you say where. And, before we part, surely you'll give me a little smack.'

'That's just what I'll do,' Calamity agreed, glancing through the mouth of the alley and deriving satisfaction from there being nobody in sight.

Shrugging herself free from the bony hands, the redhead took a step back. Knotting her right fist, she swung it with the skill and precision acquired and improved during numerous brawls which had originated in saloons when the female employees objected to her trespassing upon what they considered as being their domain. Caught at the side of the jaw with a punch powered by a muscular development hard work had strengthened to well beyond the average, Bell was pitched backwards to collide against and slide down the wall of the building at the left. Seated on the ground, her eyes glassy, she looked up into the furious face of her assailant and, despite her wits spinning, was able to hear and understand what was said.

'Our trails aren't likely to cross again,' Calamity declared and, indicative of her feelings, she was telling herself mentally that what she wanted most at that moment was to change the shirt which the woman had pawed and take a bath. 'But, happen they do, don't you come anywheres close to me, you god-damned lesbo, or I'll do a whole lot worse than just give you a *lil smack*!'

* * *

'I've always heard tell most of her sort are that way,' Belle Boyd remarked, having listened with some amusement to a sulfurous description of the meeting with Linda Bell given by Calamity Jane as soon as they were in the room she was occupying at Mrs. Lane's boarding house. Because she knew the owner had a habit—no pun intended—of paying unexpected calls, she was still wearing her disguise. Nevertheless, she contrived to lounge with an almost cat-like grace on the bed. 'In fact, I was told this particular crowd are like it by the girl you saved from being run down by the stage.'

Sitting with legs astride a chair at the dressing-table and resting her arms along the top of its back, the redhead wore a tartan shirt and a pair of Levi's pants which had the cuffs of the legs turned up a couple of inches. Both conformed to her physical contours so snugly they gave the impression of having been bought a size too small and shrunk still more during washing. Although the rendezvous with the lady outlaw was in a respectable part of the city, the whip rode in its loop at her waist. She had accepted the prohibition on wearing firearms within the city limits during the period of the election, but was disinclined to have no weapon of any kind on her person.

After parting company with Calamity, Belle had taken Ruby Wakefield to a small coffee-house where they had attracted no attention while they talked. Showing none of her earlier reluctance to accept the 'nun' as a confidant, the young woman had supplied her name and explained that losses she had sustained gambling were responsible for her behavior. Saying she would do everything possible to help Ruby out of the predicament, Belle had not explained how she intended to go about it. Nor had she mentioned that she considered she would need the support of Calamity if she was to carry out the scheme she had in mind. Instead, she had discovered Ruby was on friendly terms with a sufficiently wealthy family to make one part of her scheme possible. The willingness of the young woman to carry out the instructions was a tribute to the way in which the lady outlaw had built up her confidence and she had shown no hesitation before promising there would be no further attempt to kill herself.

Having accompanied Ruby to the expensive hotel where she was staying and where, in fact, she had made the acquaintance with the cause of her problems, Belle had had a letter written to the leader of the group saying the money to cover the promissory notes signed for the amount of her losses would be procured and handed over in exchange for them that evening in the dining-room. She had dismissed as unimportant the warning that there was no chance of the money being available for the payment, saying all that mattered was the suggestion that payment would be forthcoming was made. She also explained that the young woman should not be in the hotel all evening, and she was assured this would be the case. Before returning to her own accommodation, having learned enough to know what would be needed, the lady outlaw made a purchase which caused the owner of the cigar store in the lobby to give her a puzzled look. Making no attempt to satisfy his obvious curiosity over why a 'nun' would want three decks of cards with backs specially designed to advertize the hotel, she had taken them to her room at Mrs. Lane's boarding house and spent the time while waiting for the redhead to join her making them ready for use.

When Calamity had arrived, seeing the obvious disapproval shown by Mrs. Lane, Belle had explained in an aside deliberately pitched just loud enough to be heard by her guest, that she had been asked to come because she was a "brand to be plucked from the burning and taught the error of her ways"; a statement which prevented any objections to them going to the room. After telling her hostess what she thought of the way she had been described, which both had considered amusing even if Calamity's comment did not appear to express appreciation, the redhead was too filled with indignation over her encounter with Linda Bell to leave mentioning it until after being informed of what the lady outlaw had learned.

Although Belle had felt certain Calamity would be a willing ally in any case, albeit probably far from satisfied with the part she was assigned, the meeting with Linda Bell had assured her co-operation was even more wholehearted!

'Her name's Ruby Wakefield,' the lady outlaw continued her explanation about the girl who had tried to kill herself. 'Seems her daddy's picked up plenty of money out of selling supplies to miners further west. Made sure she had right good schooling—but it missed some of the things a rich girl ought to know and that is why she was acting the way she did when we came across her. She got to know some of that "Women's Rights Movement" bunch at the hotel where she and they are staying and, figuring they made good sense in what they're saying in the election, if not of the fuss they've been causing at other folks' gatherings, she accepted an invitation to go to what she was told would be a private meeting at a big house in the best part of town. When she arrived, she was smart enough to figure the six of them who were there were only interested in other girls, not fellers, and she was fixing to pull out. But they didn't try to force their attentions on her and one of them suggested a game of cards to pass the time while they was supposed to be waiting for their guest speaker to come to give them a talk.'

'I can close to guess the rest,' Calamity asserted, amused by the cultured southern accent coming from the less than prepossessing appearance which the lady outlaw had given to her otherwise beautiful face, 'But you talk so good, I'll let you tell me.'

'Why thank you 'most to death, you "brand to be plucked from the burning",' Belle replied. 'She thought, them looking so respectable and all, it would be whist, or maybe piquet, but it wasn't. Instead, they told her that draw poker was such a *simple* game, she'd pick it up in no time at all.'

'She picked *something* up, I'll bet!'

'That she did. In fact, she started off winning—!'

'Now that's a real *surprise.*'

'I thought it *might* be,' Belle stated dryly, aware that—while probably not able to match her own knowledge—the redhead was well versed in all aspects of gambling. 'Anyways, the game did come easy enough to her. Fact being, although she didn't let on, she'd played it for beads and stuff with her friends at school and home. Seeing as how she was doing so much winning, she didn't notice the stakes were getting higher and higher. Then her *luck* started to change for the worse.'

'And that's another surprise,' Calamity claimed in an equally sardonic tone.

'Anyways,' the lady outlaw went on. 'It wasn't long before she'd lost all the cash she had to hand and said she was ready to quit. They talked her into just one more hand and, when it was dealt, she knew enough about poker to figure she ought to be able to get at least some of her money back, provided somebody else bet along with her.'

'Which somebody did!'

'Somebody did and they seemed real *obliging.* When she said she didn't have enough money on hand to open, they told her she could sign a note for what she wanted to bet, like some of them had been doing already. So she opened for a couple of hundred, sure she'd get it back and more. Only, at first, it seemed like she'd gone too high and scared the others out. Then the dealer saw her bet and raised it five hundred.'

'That's *real* high!'

'She reckoned having four aces dealt pat made covering it worthwhile. Then, so's the other player wouldn't guess she was holding four of a kind, she figured to play cagey and threw in the spare card to draw one even though it couldn't improve her hand. When the dealer took two, which she reckoned meant drawing to threes and couldn't lick her aces even if the fourth turned up, she was certain she'd got the money and went on to make sure it would be a good enough pile to let her come out a winner.'

'How much of a good pile?'

'All told,' Belle replied somberly, 'She signed promissory notes for two thousand, five hundred!'

'Whee-dogie!' Calamity ejaculated and, despite the gravity of the situation, she could not resist darting an amused glance at the lady outlaw. 'They took her like Grant took Richmond.'

'Or like Rip Ford took those Yankees at the Battle of Palmitto Hill down back of Brownsville, Texas,' the lady outlaw countered, being an un-Reconstructed Rebel at heart. 'The trouble being, the War had ended almost a month earlier everywhere else.'

'It never ended according to some folks,' the redhead commented, eyeing her hostess in a mock pointed fashion. Then she became serious again and went on, 'So *that's* why she tried to walk under Gilhooley's stagecoach?'

'That's only *part* of it,' Belle corrected. 'There was more than just the money she owed made her act that way.'

'What else?' the redhead inquired, although her experience with Linda Bell suggested part of the answer.

'They said they'd be willing to forget the notes she signed—provided she'd join them in *everything* they get up to,' the lady outlaw answered, confirming Calamity's suspicions. 'And, the way I see it, they were wanting to get her in such a bind, should she go along, they'd have had her where they wanted her for the rest of her life, and could bleed her dry by threatening to let her folks and friends know what she'd done to pay off the bet. I've heard their stinking soft-shell kind, men and women alike, have pulled that sort of game before.'

'Those god-damned *bitches*!' the redhead spat out furiously, her right hand going to the stock of the whip and wishing it was supplemented by her Navy Colt. 'No wonder she was acting the way she did. Any decent raised gal would be scared *loco* given a stinking choice like *that.* Thing being, Belle, what're *we* going to do about them?'

'You know something, Calamity,' the lady outlaw responded gently, but there was nothing gentle in her expres-

sion. 'I thought you'd *never* ask!'

* * *

'All right, ladies,' Belle Boyd said and the disdain in her Southern drawl—which she was deliberately making even more pronounced than usual—was not entirely simulated for the character she was now playing. 'Here we go with a lesson in how to play draw poker Texas style. Which, happen I don't come out the *winner* in this game, my name's not Betty Hardin. I'm going to take you like my grand-daddy, he's *General Ole Devil Hardin,* you know, and his Texas Light Cavalry took those Yankee soldiers in Arkansas all through the War.'

Since the meeting with Calamity Jane at Mrs. Lane's boarding house, the lady outlaw had been very busy!

However, with the time just after eight o'clock in the evening, Belle was making ready to bring the plan she had outlined to the redhead to its climax!

As was suggested by the name she used, the lady outlaw was no longer disguised as a less than attractive looking nun. Making the change had presented no difficulties for her. As an aid to her various confidence tricks, which called for different types of personality to suit the respective needs of the particular role she played, she had caches of clothing and other items in the care of trusted associates at many places throughout the area of her operations.

The store she maintained in Topeka was at the home of an apparently honest businessman who was, nevertheless, a link in a chain for disposing of stolen property which had its center in the town of Mulrooney. It was only a short distance from the accommodation she had selected for that reason and also because both were in a most respectable part of the State Capital. Choosing what was required, including something supplied by her host, she had set about making the necessary alterations to her appearance. Having taken off the spectacles, removed the bulbous false nose and 'rabbit teeth', she washed away the sallow makeup and allowed her features to revert to their normal beautiful lines. However, for the purposes of her new character, she had given them an expression of imperious arrogance. The habit of the nun was replaced by clothing and jewelry which—in addition to proving her figure was as well endowed as that of Calamity—looked costly, suggesting she was possessed of considerable wealth. To complete the change, she hid her short cropped brunette hair beneath a very realistic black wig coiffured in the latest style.

With the alteration of appearance completed, the lady outlaw had wondered what Elizabeth 'Betty' Hardin—as good a friend as was Calamity Jane in spite of being both completely law-abiding—would say *if* learning of the far from likable way in which she was to be portrayed in the interests of getting to know the potential victims and inducing them to respond as was required. Working both on what she had been told by Ruby Wakefield, and by prior experience with their kind, she had put to use the knowledge of human nature so vital to the successful conducting of a confidence trick in selecting a *persona* which would arouse the acquisitive instincts of her quarry. Being aware of the paranoid hostility liberal-radicals of middle class-middle management origins felt towards Southrons, especially those who had been as prominent in the affairs of the former Confederate States as were the genuine Betty Hardin's family, she believed they would be delighted to claim one as a victim. Nor, she felt sure, would they find anything out of the ordinary about the way she intended to behave. It would, in fact, be what they expected from one of her supposed background and upbringing.

Carrying a carpetbag, and wearing a Wavelean hat and with a long yellow 'duster' coat such as was used when travelling over her other attire, Belle had timed her arrival at the hotel, where the members of the "Women's Rights Movement" were staying, to coincide with their return from disrupting a political meeting. She saw some of them watching her with interest, if not favor, particularly when she had announced loudly in the pronounced Southern drawl that she could and would willingly pay for the *very* best suite. Informed by the desk clerk that there was only one single room available, she had insisted upon making an examination before reaching a decision, and explained away her lack of baggage by stating it had been left at the Wells Fargo depot until she had made sure the accommodation would be up to her requirements.

Having attracted the attention of her quarry at the reception desk, Belle had entered the dining-room at seven o'clock and tried just as loudly to order dishes particularly favored south of the Mason-Dixon line. She had left the hat and 'duster' in the carpetbag—which had held only old newspapers supplied by the man in charge of her cache—and was clad in a mauve silk blouse with puff sleeves and a black velvet skirt which concealed her footwear. To further emphasize her "wealthy" state, yet supposedly gauche nature, she was wearing a quantity of jewelry which looked most impressive and would have been more suitable for a formal affair than just coming to have a casual evening meal at a hotel. As on her arrival at the reception desk, everything about her appearance and voice was calculated to persuade the women she was after to decide she would be an ideal victim. Therefore, she had not been surprised when she was approached by the one she knew to be their leader.

Coming to Belle's table, Mary Abbott had engaged her in conversation by starting to discuss the rights of women. Declaring she had no interest whatsoever in 'Yankee' politics, she had expressed a wish to do some gambling and, gesturing with the vanity bag she had brought downstairs, claimed it held enough money to support her desire to play for high stakes. Taking the bait, the feminist had told her of a game of draw poker which might prove satisfactory. Stating that she doubted whether she would find any worthwhile competition outside Texas for one of her skill, she had agreed to participate in a manner suggesting she considered she would be doing the other players a favor by competing.

Studying Abbott all the time they were talking, the lady outlaw felt certain the letter from Ruby Wakefield had been accepted at its face value. In her early thirties, tallish, lean and gaunt featured, with her black hair swept back into a bun, the feminist wore a black dress which did nothing to make her more attractive. Clasping a bulky black reticule on the table, she continually darted glances at the entrance to the dining-room and showed signs of annoyance, beyond that caused by the comments 'Betty Hardin' was passing, when the person she was obviously awaiting failed to put in an appearance. Therefore, knowing how best to achieve her purpose, Belle displayed what seemed like impatience to be getting involved in the promised game of poker. Her statement that she believed Abbott was "running scared" and she would have to look elsewhere for her diversion proved successful. Glaring down at the reticule, the feminist thrust back her chair and said they would get going. Asked if they would be playing in a room at the hotel, she replied that the venue was a mansion loaned by a supporter of the "Women's Rights Movement" as it offered a greater privacy.

On going to the reception desk, learning Ruby Wakefield had left the hotel earlier and was still absent, Abbott did not return to her room to leave behind the promissory notes which Belle felt sure were in her reticule, and the plan which the lady outlaw had had ready to deal with such a contingency was not required. She only delayed the departure for long enough to place all the jewelry she was wearing in the safe in the manager's office supplied for the benefit of the residents. Then she reappeared with a thick bundle of what appeared to be brand new ten dollar bills, causing an avaricious gleam to come into the feminist's eyes as she placed it in her commodious vanity bag. Having sent her companions to prepare for the game, Abbott took their intended victim to the venue in a hansom cab. What she did not know was that Calamity Jane was following in another which was driven by an acquaintance of Cecil 'Dobey' Killem and who had offered his services for the evening without asking any questions.

The mansion to which Belle was taken stood in its own grounds, surrounded by a high wall. Passing along the wide path to the front entrance, passing through a garden with a number of bushes decorating well cared for lawns, she noticed only one room at the front showed any sign of occupancy. Just beyond where a fair sized cottonwood tree was growing, a light glowed through a set of French windows beyond a balustrade and porch over which was a balcony for the rooms on the unlit second floor. Commenting upon the otherwise deserted aspect of the building, she was told this was because the owners were away on vacation and had given the "Women's Rights Movement" permission to use it in their absence for holding meetings with sympathizers. Wondering whether this was correct and feeling sure the offer did not include running a dishonest poker game with blackmail as its eventual object, the lady outlaw did not take the matter any further. However, she considered its lack of occupants other than the women against whom she would be in contention and the comparative isolation of the property made it just as well suited to her purpose as theirs.

Passing through the gloomy entrance hall and into the large dining-room, illuminated by two large crystal chande-liers, Belle found the other five members of the group which had cheated Ruby Wakefield were seated at the table in the center and were trying to give the impression that they had been playing for some time. Studying their behavior, she concluded it would not have fooled anybody with the slightest experience of crooked gambling. Not, she also reminded herself, that their victims had been in such a category until she had caused herself to be selected.

Making sure she had obtained the seat at the left of Abbott, while being introduced to the others, the lady outlaw had subjected each to a scrutiny and assessment of the respective potential they possessed in what she felt sure would follow. If it did not, she had thought with some amusement, Calamity would be even more disappointed than herself. Judging from their appearances, she could imagine why each had elected to become a feminist and discard association with men. Their hair was done in unflattering styles and their clothes were intended to prevent any suggestion of their figures showing. Not one had an appearance likely to find favor with members of the opposite sex.

If the redhead's pungent description had not been sufficient for Belle, the bruise on the jaw of the woman at Abbott's right would have identified her as Linda Bell. Next came the biggest of them, almost six foot tall, bulky and surly faced Merle Amory. Except for one being a blonde and the other a redhead, Jill Forbes and Margaret Gascoigne were sufficiently alike in size, build, narrow and sharp, unpleasant features to be Abbott's sisters. About six inches shorter than Amory, Louise Anderson had the build of a badly made plum pudding and the lady outlaw considered she looked nearly as intelligent, which was not saying much.

Noticing all of the women were wearing rings which would make effective weapons when the trouble she anticipated erupted, Belle had caused them to be removed. Claiming that as she had heard of devices being fitted to them as an aid to marking cards, she had deliberately left her own rings behind as an indication of good faith, she insisted that while she felt sure nothing of the kind would be attempted—in a manner which implied she did—she expected the other players to show a similar respect for the game. Despite their protests, seeing she was adamant and being led to assume she would leave the game if not humored, the feminists did as she wished and placed the rings they took off in their reticules on their laps. However, she had not been able to find a counter when Abbott said the drapes must be drawn across the French windows to prevent anybody seeing the game was taking place. Although this would mean Calamity could not watch what was happening, Belle drew consolation from the night being sufficiently warm for the transom at the top to be left open to allow in a cooling breeze.

Having achieved all she wanted, with the exception of the shades, the lady outlaw was ready to put the remainder of her scheme into operation and made the declaration which she did not doubt would cause the women to be even more determined to get her in their power.

* * *

'Well, that's all the cash I have with me,' Belle Starr announced in a tone suggestive of bitterness. 'So I'm going to finish.'

'I haven't been doing so well either,' Merle Amory rumbled in her deep, almost man-like voice. 'So I'll go out and see if there's a hansom we can use to go back to the hotel.'

'Why not have another hand while she's looking, Betty?' Mary Abbott inquired, gathering up and starting to shuffle the cards, as the big woman rose and lumbered away with all the grace of a particularly clumsy hippopotamus.

'I just told you that I don't have any more money with me,' the lady outlaw pointed out sullenly.

'Then do like you've seen some of the other girls do,' Abbott suggested. 'Sign a promissory note and, if you lose, make it good when you get back to the hotel.'

The game of draw poker had gone on for just over an hour. While it was taking place, Belle had satisfied herself she was not up against skilled card manipulators. In fact, had she wished, she could have taken them for all the money they had with them by putting her own training in that field to use. Instead, she had given a most convincing performance of possessing a little ability which was only dangerous to herself. Wondering whether the opposition had sufficient card savvy to appreciate what she was doing, she had sought to convey the impression of one trying to prove herself much more knowledgeable and being better at playing draw poker than was really the case. What was more, to ensure her actions at the appropriate moment did not come as a surprise and arouse comment, she had insisted upon patting the remainder of the deck 'for luck'—using a twisting motion of her left hand to display it was empty—every time before she was given the number of cards she asked to 'draw'.

At first, as had happened when Ruby Wakefield was the victim, the feminists had done everything they could—such as claiming to have been beaten by what was actually an inferior hand—to ensure a suitable frame of mind by allowing their 'unsuspecting victim' to win. Even when they sought to change her 'luck', which was genuinely good and which none possessed the necessary manipulative ability to change, on several occasions she had had to discard hands capable of taking the pot if she had gone to a showdown. While being allowed to win, she had acted happy and, to supply a further inducement for the feminists to believe she could be made the subject of blackmail, boasted of how her grandfather, 'General Ole Devil Hardin, you know', had entrusted her with a very large sum of

money to deliver to a business associate in Topeka. She had also committed 'errors of judgment' which encouraged them to believe they were achieving their purpose. Playing her part perfectly, when the 'reverses' to her fortunes began to take toll, she had behaved in what seemed to be a more reckless fashion which helped reduce her finances to the point where the completely dishonest ploy could be performed.

'All right, I'll do that,' Belle agreed.

'Put your full name and address at the top, then write I.O.U. and the sum and sign it,' Abbott instructed, fetching a notepad, pen and bottle of ink from a drawer in the sidepiece. 'It's only a formality which is *always* done when playing poker, as you must know, Hard-*Betty.*'

'Why sure, we do it *all* the time back home to Texas,' the lady outlaw answered in the tone of one trying to prove a non-existent experience to match that which she believed the other players possessed. Taking the pen, she wrote, *'Elizabeth Hardin, OD Connected Ranch, Rio Hondo County, Texas'* in a childish scrawl. Then what passed for a crafty expression came to her face and she continued, 'I'll fill the amount in *after* I've seen my cards.'

'Of course,' Abbott agreed. 'Cut the deck and we'll get on with the game.'

'Cut light, lose all night's been working,' Belle said bitterly, splitting the pile of cards well below the halfway point. 'So I'll go deeper this time.'

'Let's hope it improves your luck,' Abbott replied. Directing a pointed glance and nod at Linda Bell, she swung her gaze across the room and went on, 'Why it's Amory back already!'

"Sorry, Hardin!' the biggest of the feminists boomed. 'There isn't a hansom anywhere to be seen.'

Knowing she was expected to fall victim to the distraction, Belle had obligingly looked around even before hearing her 'name'. She had no need to keep Abbott and Bell under observation to know they were changing the cards she had seen shuffled and cut herself for another deck which was suitably prepared supplied from the latter's reticule. Being certain this had happened, without needing to so much as glance down, she dropped her hands into her lap and made the necessary preparations for coping with the situation. Then she sat back with an air of unsuspecting innocence and watched the new cards being dealt.

'I'll put you in, Amory,' Abbott announced. 'Then we'll make this the *last* hand and we'll all go back to the hotel in the carriage you girls used to come out here.'

Paying no attention to the mutter of concurrence from the other feminists, apart from realizing it was to put her in the required mood for what lay immediately ahead, Belle picked up and looked at five cards which would have gladdened the heart of a genuine player in the position she had allowed herself to reach. Keeping up her performance as the pretended authority who was really far from experienced or competent, she allowed the kind of intake of breath she suspected had been given by most of the previous victims at the sight of the four aces she was dealt pat. 'Is there a *limit* to what we can bet?' the lady outlaw inquired with well simulated eagerness.

'Certainly not,' Abbott declared and flickered a glance of triumph at the other feminists.

'I'll open for one—three—*five* hundred!' Belle announced, even though aware that the choice should have been

with the player at the right of the dealer and progress around the others before she spoke. Laying down the cards and grabbing the pen, she continued excitedly, 'I'll fill in the rest of the amounts on the promissory note as I bet them.'

'That's fine with us,' Abbott asserted as the writing was commenced, also disregarding the correct order of betting in her eagerness to get the better of the beautiful Southern girl who had aroused her envy and hatred for having attributes she lacked. Directing another triumphant look at her companions and starting to count out the money, she added, 'I'll see you and raise you five hundred!'

'That's *far* too much for *me,* Abbott!' Bell claimed, tossing her cards to the center of the table.

'And me,' Amory grunted, repeating the disposal. 'I might just as well not have joined in again.'

'I'm out,' Jill Forbes declared.

'And me,' Margaret Gascoigne supported.

'Not with what I've got,' Louise Anderson stated, also throwing her hand into the discards.

'It looks like it's left between just you two, Hardin, Abbott.'

'So it does,' Belle agreed, with what passed as relief that she had opposition to benefit her very powerful hand. 'I'll see that five hundred and raise it the same.'

'You must have *good* cards!' Abbott commented, almost sounding as if she did not know the exact value of the hand held by her intended victim. Pushing forward the appropriate amount from the money before her, she went on, 'Well, so have I and I believe that if you have them, play them. I'll have to see that five. How many cards do you want?'

'Two,' the lady outlaw answered, tossing the ace of spades and nine of clubs face down among the discards with a well produced smirk of triumph.

'Don't you want to pat the cards for luck?' Abbott inquired with just a hint of mockery and, showing no signs of surprise at the decision, refrained from picking up the unused portion of the deck.

'Wha-Oh *yes,* of course!' Belle ejaculated, having taken up the pen with her right hand as if impatient to carry on betting. Reaching out, still conveying the impression of being wanting to resume the game and collect the winnings she anticipated, she tapped the remainder of the deck without having first made the twisting motion which she had done previously to establish her left palm was empty. Snatching it back, as soon as she received the top two cards and looked at them, she continued, 'I'll open for five hundred!'

'You definitely *must* have improved your hand,' Abbott commented and again sent a smirk of satisfaction around the table. 'I'll take two as well. Perhaps we're both after the same thing?'

'It could be,' Belle drawled and glanced at the drapes across the French windows. Still simulating the eagerness of one convinced she had the winning hand, she went on, 'Well, what are you going to do?'

'How much are you willing to go for?' Abbott inquired, without troubling to examine the two cards she gave herself.

Once before when using the ploy, the intended victim had evidently heard of it and sought to nullify the effect by discarding an ace and the fifth card. However, the man from whom Abbott had learned of the trick had warned this might happen and supplied a counter for such attempts at nullifica-

tion. When preparing the deck, she gave herself the nine, ten, jack of hearts and two valueless cards. However, on top of the remainder were the seven, eight, queen and king of hearts to take care of any contingency. Generally the victim would draw one card, hoping to make it appear she was trying to fill a flush or straight. In which case, the eight and queen would supply a straight flush. If she tried as had 'Betty Hardin' to completely ruin the ploy by taking two, the queen and king would still be available to produce the powerful hand which would even have beaten the four aces.

'I can cover everything on the table, yours and theirs, with the money I was given to pay off—I left at the hotel,' the lady outlaw claimed. 'Why not get them to loan you theirs and we'll have a showdown for it all?'

'Why not?' Abbott agreed, noticing the way the first part of the comment was amended and delighted by the possibilities for blackmail she felt sure were being offered. 'If they don't mind lending me their money, that is?'

'You can have mine,' Bell confirmed and, being equally aware of what was to come despite the attempt of the 'Texan' to circumvent the ploy, the other four were just as eager to comply.

'That comes to fifteen hundred dollars,' Abbott announced, showing no concern over the money she was using being the funds supplied by the people sponsoring the "Women's Rights Movement" for attending the election and disrupting opposition politicians. 'And, with what you've already bet, you'll be signing the promissory note for over two thousand.'

'That's all right with me,' Belle declared with complete truth. 'And, while I'm writing out the promissory note, will you separate the new bills I brought so nobody will get to know I've used the—so I can put them back—! I mean, it will save time when I w-!'

'Don't worry, we *know* what you mean,' Abbott replied, more convinced than ever that the loss of the money entrusted to 'Betty Hardin's' care anticipated by all the feminists would put her completely in their power and savoring the humiliations they would heap upon her. 'We'll only be too pleased to do *everything* we can for *you*.'

'Well, that's *that*!' the lady outlaw asserted, having taken sufficient time for the separation to be completed while filling in the designated sum of money beneath the name and address she had supplied. 'Let's play poker!'

'What do you have?' Abbott inquired, wanting to make the beautiful Southern girl suffer as much as possible when the showdown took place.

'Full house, aces and tens!' Belle replied, turning her cards face up on the table and starting to whistle "Dixie" loudly.

high' and, under the unexpected circumstances, completely worthless hand. 'I-I-I shouldn't have *these* two—!'

'Now how would a player in an *honest* game know *that*?' the lady outlaw asked in her normal tone, having stopped the whistling and tensed on her seat.

The difference in the way "Betty Hardin" spoke while posing the question brought every eye from the exposed cards to her. Considering the benefits in upbringing and education each had been given by their respectively indulgent middle class-middle management parents, which had imbued little more than an over-inflated sense of what was actually non-existent personal superiority and brilliance, not one of the feminists could be termed bright or particularly perceptive. However, all of them were able to discern the change which had come over their intended victim. The realization that her earlier naive behavior had been nothing more than a successful pose, adopted to outwit and turn the tables

'Fu—?' Abbott gurgled and snatched up her own cards for the first time since completing the draw. To her horror, instead of the expected queen and king of hearts, to provide a straight flush and defeat the full house which should not be confronting her, she found she had replaced the two valueless cards from her hand with the four of clubs and six of spades for a 'jack

on them, came almost simultaneously. That it was achieved by a woman with such obviously Southern origins and who had the beauty and physical attractions they lacked and envied, while pretending to despise such attributes, made the discovery even more galling for each of them.

'She's *tricked* us!' Bell screeched, shoving back her chair and starting to stand up while pointing an accusatory finger at Belle.

'The peckerwood bitch *knew* what to *expect*!' Amory said at the same moment, watching the lady outlaw starting to thrust their money—but not the new bills-into her vanity bag.

'She had *cards palmed* and put them on the deck when she touched it for *luck*!' Abbott assessed correctly, the four having been extracted without detection earlier and retained beneath the vanity bag on Belle's lap. 'Come on, girls. Let's teach her a *lesson* she'll *never* forget!'

'There's only one thing I can say to *that*!' Belle declared mockingly, using sufficient force in thrusting back her chair to ensure she was able to rise and move away from the table without impediment. As the rest of the feminists also began to come to their feet and move towards her, tossing the now bulging vanity bag on to the sidepiece near a bowl containing artificial fruit, she raised her voice in a yell. 'Hey, *CALAMITY*!'

* * *

Seeing the drapes being drawn at the french windows while she was advancing cautiously through the bushes towards the mansion, Calamity Jane had shared Belle Starr's misgivings. Taking advantage of the occupants being unable to look outside, she had crossed the porch and gently tried the handles. Finding the lock and bolts were secured, she had realized the disadvantage she was facing. Glancing around, she decided there was a way in which she might be able to see what was happening and be ready to lend the assistance she had agreed upon with the lady outlaw when the climax of the game was reached. Although the

rest of the lower branches had been removed, one sufficiently sturdy to support a children's swing was left on the cottonwood tree just beyond the balustrade. It was parallel to the house and at a sufficient height for her to be able to keep watch through the uncovered and open transom. Climbing up, aided by the ropes of the swing, had proved easy enough and was accomplished without making enough noise to be heard inside the dining-room.

Standing on the limb and finding she was able to see most of the table at which the game would take place, the redhead had watched the feminists being compelled to remove and put away their rings. The sight gave her satisfaction. Until meeting the lady outlaw, she had been anticipating a boring visit to Topeka. Because of the delicate state of affairs caused by the election, being all too aware of her penchant for becoming involved in brawls and other unruly incidents, her employer had given orders that she must keep out of trouble.

Watching the game commence, Calamity was pleased with the way things had turned out. Knowing he was a firm believer in justice being done—even if not in a strictly legal fashion—she was convinced Dobey Killem would approve of what she was doing should he hear about it. There was certain to be physical opposition when the truth about "Betty Hardin" was revealed and she was looking forward to tangling with the women who had almost caused Ruby Wakefield to commit suicide. Studying them, despite realizing they would have the advantage of numbers on their side, she had felt no qualms over having being compelled to leave her gunbelt and Navy Colt behind. When the time came, she told herself as she squatted on her haunches to await developments, there would be the satisfaction of dealing out punishment with her bare hands and any other way required in excess of that already inflicted upon Bell.

Rising to her feet at intervals, Calamity had kept the progress of the game under observation. Although she was seated when the 'distraction' allowed Mary Abbott to change the decks, hearing "Dixie" being whistled and knowing only the lady outlaw would select that particular tune, caused her to get up. Having already decided how to make her entrance, she balanced herself on the branch and started to put the idea into effect. Bringing the whip from its belt loop, she caused the lash to uncoil behind her and sent it forward and upwards. By the kind of coincidence no author of fiction would dare employ in a plot, Belle yelling her name came at the same instant as the explosive crack of the lash and prevented it from being heard by the feminists.

While giving the shout for assistance, the lady outlaw was also making ready for action on her own behalf. To facilitate doing so, she put to use a modification to her attire which she had learned from another good and law abiding woman friend, Belle 'the Rebel Spy' Boyd. Giving a tug at the fastening of the waistband, she caused it to open out. Set free, the black velvet skirt fell downwards to show she had on brown riding breeches and boots instead of conventional feminine undergarments and footwear. Stepping clear, she lashed around a backhand blow to the face which spun Mary Abbott away from her. However, she felt herself grabbed by the shoulder from behind. Before she could retaliate, Louise Anderson gave her a surging shove and she was propelled in a sprawl against the sidepiece. A glance to her rear warned that her assailant and the other feminists were moving in her direction.

Curling out as directed, the end of the whip's lash wrapped around the top of the guardrail for the upstairs' balcony. Giving a tug to ensure it was sufficiently tight for her needs, Calamity grasped the handle in both hands and, first jumping to the rear, launched herself from her perch. Swinging downwards, under the impulsion of the pendulous effect her weight gave to the tightly stretched and strong plaited leather, she lifted her legs so they passed over the top of the porch's balustrade. Arriving with the full force of her shapely and powerful body behind them, her feet struck the framework where the two parts of the French windows came together. The impact burst them inwards to the accompaniment of splintering wood and breaking glass. Having released the handle, she plummeted onwards into the room and alighted in a kneeling posture with arms thrown behind her as an aid to retaining balance.

Hearing the commotion, all the feminists came to a halt and looked around. Linda Bell realized the newcomer was the redhead with whom she had tried to become more than just casually acquainted instead of continuing her task of following to make sure Ruby Wakefield did not go to lodge a complaint with the local peace officers. Aroused by the thought of how she was spurned when she had made the proposition, she gave a screech like a scalded cat. Forgetting what had happened, she rushed across the room with her hands extended to grab hair. It was not, anybody who knew her proposed victim could have warned, the wisest or most effective action she could have carried out.

Thrusting herself towards the approaching feminist, Calamity did not straighten from the crouching posture. Instead, her head passed beneath the reaching fingers and rammed into Bell's midsection. Thrown backwards with all the air driven from her lungs, the stricken woman folded at the waist and dropped to her knees. However, as she went, Margaret Gascoigne had concluded the newcomer was not there by chance nor to aid the cause of the "Women's Rights Movement" and, electing to leave dealing with "Betty Hardin" to the others, was dashing to the attack.

Snatching up the bowl of artificial fruit from near her vanity bag, Belle twisted around and flung its contents into Anderson's face. Having done so, she gave her attention to the next nearest of her intended assailants. Taking a warning from what happened to Abbott, Jill Forbes allowed Amory to pass her. Lumbering up, the massive woman hurled a punch at the lady outlaw. However, while the fist was propelled by all her weight and undoubted power, it was slow and 'telegraphed' to one with Belle's considerable experience in such matters. Swiveling onwards from dealing with Anderson, she deftly interposed the sturdy metal bowl so it

and not her face was struck by the approaching knuckles. A yelp of pain burst from Amory and, before she could recover from the shock, a foot was rammed against her stomach to thrust her backwards. Despite having removed the biggest of the feminists, Belle was not to be given a respite. Abbott, Anderson and Forbes were all converging upon her.

Straightening up, Calamity caught Gascoigne by the wrist and, stepping aside, gave a swinging heave which propelled her across the room. Then, seeing Belle was about to be attacked by the three feminists, she set about rendering assistance. Darting forward, she bounded on to and dived across the table. Flying through the air, she threw an arm around the necks of Abbott and Forbes while passing between them. Coming down on her feet, causing her captives to reel and bend at the waist, she sought to retain her hold long enough for the lady outlaw to deal with the third would-be attacker and take action against them.

Ignoring her companions' problems, Anderson sent her fingers into what she imagined to be stylishly coiffured black hair and gave a savage jerk at it. However, the attack did not meet the response she anticipated. Before she could realize the locks she was grasping were artificial, they came away in her hands without causing the recipient of the attack either pain or inconvenience. In fact, the only one to suffer from it was Anderson. Caught by a roundhouse punch to the jaw which proved her assailant to be as competent as the red haired intruder, letting the wig fall from her hands as she went, she was sent in a twirling sprawl across the room.

Realizing she would need covering for her head and wanting to keep the wig from being damaged, Belle kicked it under the sidepiece before doing anything else. Then, turning, she found Calamity was still holding Abbott and Forbes in the side head-locks. Struggling to get free from the choking grip, they were pulling her head back by its shortish red locks and digging fingers into the inside of her thighs in what—despite the sturdy blue material of the Levi's pants—was obviously an equally painful fashion. In fact, the punishment they were inflicting had the desired effect, if not quite as they would have wished. Letting out a pungent profanity, Calamity gave a surging upwards heave and removed her arms to send the pair away from her in a spinning stumble. Advancing to help the redhead, Belle interlocked her fingers and swung them to catch Forbes at the side of the jaw. Although she knocked the feminist staggering, as she was about to follow up the blow, Amory was rushing at her. Bending at the waist before the outstretched hands could sieze her, she straightened as the biggest feminist collided against her and tipped forward. Made to perform an involuntary half somersault over her intended victim, Amory descended with a thud upon the thick carpet covering the floor.

The fight raged with unabated fury for over five minutes. Throughout it, superiority in numbers was all the feminists had in their favor. Driven by fury and a mutual desire to take revenge upon the Southern girl who had made such fools of them, their efforts were completely without cohesion and they got in one another's way to the benefit of their opponents. What was more, they were up against two women in the peak of physical condition and who respectively possessed considerable knowledge of wrestling, fist fighting and all-in brawling.

There was not a second when fists and feet were still instead of being used with complete impartiality. In addition, hair was grabbed at and pulled. However, although the shortish locks of Calamity and Belle were far less susceptible than those of their antagonists—particularly as the buns disintegrated—generally they preferred more effective methods of attack. Almost incessantly, whether from their punches, kicks, pushes, or a variety of wrestling throws, one or another of the the feminists was sent staggering and sprawling, or flipped through the air to alight with varying degrees of impact. Clutching fingers damaged clothes, but the attire of the opposition offered far greater scope than the more snugly fitting garments worn by Belle and Calamity. All had their blouses torn to varying degrees and not one of the feminists' skirts survived undamaged. Pulled from the waistband of the Levi's pants, in addition to having all the buttons ripped off, the redhead's shirt lost a sleeve.

Not everything went in favor of the redhead and Belle. At times one, the other, or both were in difficulties. However, on each occasion, the skill possessed by whichever was in trouble helped her to escape, or her friend came to her assistance. Therefore, as a result of their individual and combined efforts, aided by the ineptitude of the feminists—all of whom were engaged for the first time in physical conflict—at last Calamity and the lady outlaw were getting the better of the fracas.

Moving forward to attack Belle, who was caught around the arms from behind by Forbes, Gascoigne was thwarted. Bringing up her feet, the lady outlaw rammed them into the red haired feminist's chest and gave a thrust which caused the blonde to stagger and let go. Precipitated backwards and losing her balance, Gascoigne went down with her head cracking against the sidepiece hard enough to render her *hors de combat.* She was the first of her group to be put out of action by only a slight margin. Pivoting fast, Belle brought off an uppercut which took Forbes under the chin and knocked her out as effectively as her predecessor. She crashed spread-eagled on the floor.

Having lost her skirt, bringing into view long legged white cotton knickers and spindly calves, Linda Bell was shoved on to the table by Anderson who was trying to get at Belle. Coming to her feet, she saw Calamity was being punched in the stomach by Amory.

'How do *you* like being hit in the gut!' the redhead yelled, twisting at the torso and delivering a much more effective blow.

As the fist sank almost wrist deep into her midsection, if the reaction from Amory was any guide, she did not like it. Her eyes and cheeks bulged out as all the air was driven from her lungs in a belching squawk. Clutching at the point of impact with both hands, she collapsed winded and helpless to her knees. At the sight of her particular friend being treated in such a fashion, especially as it was done by the redhead she already had cause to hate, Linda Bell screeched and threw herself bodily from the table. More by chance than deliberately, she tilted sideways with the intention of crashing into and knocking Calamity face down to the floor. However, the yell had been an error in tactics and the redhead swung around instead of being caught from the rear. What was more, as the slender body arrived against her torso, she had the weight and strength to withstand the hoped for effect.

Before Linda Bell could drop to the floor, she was grabbed by the throat with Calamity's right hand and the other was slipped between her thighs to grasp the waistband of her knickers. Deftly twisting her writhing captive from horizontal to vertical, the redhead turned and stepped to where Amory was still kneeling and showing the distress caused by the punch to the stomach. Raising Linda Bell, undeterred by her wildly waving arms and legs, Calamity swung her downwards so the top of her head slammed against that of the biggest feminist. Rendered unconscious, Amory keeled over backwards and, on being released, Bell flopped down to alight supine and just as flaccidly across her bulky torso. Having put two more of the feminists out of the fight, tackled around the waist by Abbott, Calamity was brought down. They went rolling across the floor struggling furiously, to end with the redhead's legs wrapped around and crushing at the leader of the group's head. Retaining the scissor-hold, despite the writhing and kicking its recipient was doing in an attempt to escape, Calamity looked around. Not too far away, Belle and Anderson had their fingers interlocked and they were engaged in an instinctive trial of strength. What was more, having contrived to take a less active part in the conflict than her companions, Anderson was able to match the strength of the lady outlaw. In fact, because of the exertions to which Belle had been subjected, she was finding herself in something close to a stalemate.

Glancing around while continuing the constriction she was applying to Abbott's head, Calamity decided to help the lady outlaw. Opening her legs, she rolled away from her captive to grab and jerk at Anderson's ankles. Alarmed by the attack, the bulky feminist could not help relaxing the efforts she was making with her arms. Snatching her hands free, Belle lashed up her right leg. Anderson's skirt had been torn down the front and was flapping open, so the foot had nothing to impede it as it rose between her thighs and struck the bottom of her knickers.

Although her assailant had been unable to attain the power which could have been employed earlier in the fight, she clasped at the vulnerable point of her anatomy and, doubling at the waist, turned away gasping in pain.

Taking advantage of Calamity being distracted, Abbott began to rise with the intention of running from the room. She was not allowed to carry out her plan. Instead of following up the attack on Anderson, Belle darted over to grab the leader of the group by her sweat matted and tangled black hair. Jerked erect, Abbott received a punch in the stomach which folded her at the middle. Then her head was grabbed and encircled by the lady outlaw's left arm. While this was happening, Calamity had got up and caught Anderson in the same fashion. Converging at a run and dragging their captives after them, they caused the tops of the protruding heads to be rammed together with a click like two giant billiard balls making contact. Jolted free by the collision, Abbott and Anderson toppled on to their backs and, after each's body had writhed spasmodically for a moment, went limp.

* * *

'L-Looks like they're *all* plumb tuckered out,' Calamity Jane gasped, glancing around and sounding just a trifle disappointed.

'L-Looks that way,' Belle Starr confirmed, after sucking in a few deep breaths. Studying the sprawled out feminists, all of whom had either bloody noses or other injuries acquired in the conflict, she went on, 'Your face is a mite redder than usual, but it's not marked up like some of them are. How about me?'

'You've come through it without getting more than a touch mussed up,' the redhead assessed. 'What now?'

'I want to take a look in Abbott's bag,' Belle replied. 'Will you collect all the cards we were using.'

'Sure,' the redhead assented and, starting to do as she was told, went on, 'How about this money?'

'Leave the new stuff,' the lady outlaw answered and went to pick up Abbott's reticule. Opening the envelope she extracted, she looked at the contents. 'I thought she'd have Ruby Wakefield's promissory notes with her, but this's even *better*!'

'How come?' Calamity asked, without interrupting the task of gathering the cards used in the final hand and the money belonging to the feminists which Belle had not had time to put in her reticule.

'She's got the rest they've tricked other girls into signing with her,' the lady outlaw explained, guessing correctly that Abbott had been too mistrusting to leave such items in the safe at the hotel. Picking up the pen, notepad and inkwell which had been knocked to the floor along with the cards and money during the fighting, she found there was still enough ink left for her purpose. 'I'm leaving them a warning that I'm sending the notes to the girls who've been slickered saying they should put the law on them. Likely none of the girls will want to let it be found out what happened, so won't do it; but Abbott and her crowd are going to be as worried as hell in case one or more of them should do it.'

'They deserve to be more than just *worried,* but we'll likely have to settle for just that,' Calamity declared. 'Anyways, I've got all the cards. What now?'

'You'll find three decks in my vanity bag,' Belle replied. 'Throw one over the floor like those you picked up were and put the others into this bag of Abbott's.'

'Yo!' the redhead assented. 'Mind telling me why?'

'I'm going to have Mick tell the first lawman he sees that he heard a ruckus here and, knowing the folks who own it are away, reckons it should be looked into.'

'That's smart figuring, but why'd we need to change the cards?'

'Happen the lawman we send looks careful, which I reckon he will, he'll find they're *marked.* I've made sure of *that.* Then he's going to start asking questions that could delay him getting somebody to come after us.'

'It's your game and I'll play it out, even if we *both* wind up in the pokey,' Calamity declared. 'But it seems a pity to leave them all this money.'

'You'd be likely to wind up "in the pokey" if you took it and tried to spend it,' the lady outlaw replied, waving the sheet of paper upon which she had written to dry the ink. 'They're all *forgeries* I bought cheap for the game.'

'There's only one lil thing,' Calamity commented, as the other preparations for departure were being completed. Anticipating there would be a fight, she had not brought her kepi and was doing what she could to make her damaged shirt presentable for being viewed outside the building. Having replaced the discarded skirt, Belle was donning the wig retrieved from beneath the sidepiece. 'I know it's only till you can get to the bag you gave me to bring along and ole Mick won't say nothing, 'though I reckon he'll *enjoy* the view, but you'll sure have anybody's might see us leaving looking at you kind of *curious* and, way this high-toned end of town'll be watched over, that lawman you're wanting could be one of them.'

'Well now,' Belle replied, aware the blouse and silk shift beneath it had been torn so badly they could no longer conceal her bosom. 'I'd never have thought of that. Come on, I saw the bunch who were here when I arrived had left their hats and coats on the stand by the front door and I'll use one of them.'

Glancing around and satisfying themselves that none of the feminists were showing signs of recovery, Calamity and the lady outlaw left the room. Crossing the entrance hall, Belle collected a shawl from the attire put on the stand by the women who had meant to cheat her. Wrapping it around her shoulders, she looked through one of the glass panels in the front door and an annoyed exclamation burst from her.

'What's up?' the redhead asked.

'There're lawmen coming without

Mick needing to send them!' Belle replied.

'It was that bunch back there's was trying to slicker *you,'* Calamity pointed out, gazing through the second panel. A sergeant and two patrolmen, wearing the uniform of the Topeka Police Department, were approaching along the path in a buckboard. 'Not t'other way 'round—for *once.'*

'A body would think I go around slickering folks all the time, way you talk,' the lady outlaw protested, amused by the way the comment had ended and replying in kind, despite having a better appreciation of how the situation had changed due to the unexpected arrival of the peace officers. 'But I don't want to be asked to explain *our* part in it, especially with the marked cards and forged money back there.'

'Nor me, comes to that!' Calamity conceded.

'Could you get away without being seen if you went through those French windows you busted?' Belle asked.

'I've snuck by Injuns when needed and'm still wearing my hair!'

'Go to it then!'

'How about *you*?'

'I've talked my way by lawmen when needed and never wound up making hair bridles in a jail,' Belle replied, not displeased by her friend's concern for her welfare and referring to a task frequently carried out by prisoners in Western penitentiaries. 'Get going and leave me do it again!'

Accepting the lady outlaw was far more experienced than herself in such matters, Calamity did as she was instructed. Hurrying through the dining-room, where a couple of the feminists were beginning to stir—although, she noticed with relief, neither had recovered sufficiently to be able to do any-

thing which might attract the attention of the peace officers—she looked out of the French windows cautiously and jerked back her head almost immediately. It seemed that getting away would not be as simple as she had envisaged. The buckboard was halted in front of the main entrance and, although she felt sure that she had not been seen, the sergeant was pointing in her direction. Wondering if he had noticed the damaged door despite the drapes having fallen back into place after she went through, or seen her whip hanging from the upstairs balcony, she turned and darted back across the room. However, before she could go into the entrance hall, she saw the lady outlaw was opening the front door and stopped in her tracks to listen.

'Th-Thank *heavens* you've come, officers!' Belle gasped, adopting a Mid-West accent which seemed to be quavering with alarm and fear.

'What's up, lady!' a deep masculine voice demanded from outside the building.

Deciding the lady outlaw had seen

what was happening and was trying to create a diversion which would prevent a man being sent to investigate whatever had attracted the attention of the sergeant, Calamity swung around. Running to the French windows and easing between the drapes, a glance informed her that both patrolmen were following the sergeant through the front door. Going outside, she grabbed the handle of her whip and shook it free. Crossing the porch, with the lash trailing behind her like a long tail, she vaulted the balustrade and darted silently to the nearest bushes. Crouching in concealment, coiling the lash, she turned her attention to the front door and watched how Belle was coping with the unanticipated development.

'I-In there!' the lady outlaw gasped, concealing her relief at the way her appearance was preventing the patrolman being sent to the French windows.

'What's in there?' the sergeant inquired, as he and his companions gazed across the entrance hall instead of behind them.

'I-I was asked to come here to attend a meeting of the "Women's Rights Movement",' Belle explained in a breathless fashion, watching the redhead taking cover without being detected. 'B-But they tried to get me into a game of poker and-and-!'

'Yes, ma'am?' the sergeant prompted, darting a glance at the patrolmen.

'One of them was caught using marked cards by the others,' Belle obliged. 'Th-Then a f-fight started—a *real* one, not just shouting and arguing-and-and I was so *afraid.* In fact, one of them *attacked* me and to-tore my b-blouse.'

'Take it easy, ma'am!' the sergeant said and his companions mumbled just as sympathetically. 'You're safe *now.* We're here and'll 'tend to them. From what you say, it looks like that letter we got saying them Women's women bunch're running a crooked poker game here's right. Come back in and sit dow—!'

'I-I don't want to go into that room again!' the lady outlaw interrupted, speaking the complete truth even though not for the reason which the three peace officers were drawing. 'In fact, I want to get out of this house. I-I'm staying next door with my Uncle Winston, that's *Senator Dillwater* you know, and won't feel *safe* until I'm back there.'

'I'll come with you, ma'am,' the taller of the patrolmen offered and the other repeated the suggestion at almost the same moment.

'Y-You'll *all* be needed to deal with *them,'* Belle replied, pointing behind her. 'I'll go through the gate in the garden wall as I did when I came here and wait for you there. I'm *sure* Uncle Winston will want to thank you for coming just in time.'

'It'd be best if you wait here, ma'am,' the sergeant suggested, wanting to be sure it was he and not one of his subordinates received whatever praise was forthcoming for looking after Senator Winston Dillwater's niece. 'We'll tend to those gals and then *I'll* go with you.'

'W-Whatever you say,' Belle assented, going to flop rather than just sit on a chair by the hall stand. 'Go and do your duty, gentlemen, and I'm sure my uncle will be most grateful when I tell him what you've done.'

'They're all down and out, serge,' the taller of the patrolmen announced, having strode to the door of the dining-room. The feminists had caused the Police Department a great deal of trouble during the election campaign and a note of satisfaction came into his voice as he continued, 'Why don't we go fetch some buckets of water from the kitchen and douse 'em to bring 'em 'round?'

'Do you think that is *wise,* sergeant?' Belle inquired. 'From what Uncle Winston has told me about the owner of this house, he won't take it kindly that his carpet was ruined by policemen, no matter how good your reason.'

'The lady's right about that, serge,' the second patrolman supported, knowing the owner was a lawyer whose political aspirations made him hostile to peace officers, 'he's *allus* against us.'

'You don't need to tell me *that,*' the sergeant asserted. 'Leave 'em to come 'round their own way. Don't even touch 'em, or they're likely to claim you was mauling their bodies all promiscuous and lewd, same's their kind's been doing every time we've had to fetch 'em away from where they was causing trouble. Let's take a look at the cards and we can talk to them when they've come 'round on their own.'

'You sure you'll be all right, ma'am?' the shorter patrolman inquired solicitously.

'Yes,' Belle confirmed. 'I'll stay here until you've finished and I feel it would be advisable for you all to be together so that you can serve as witnesses to one another's actions if those *dreadful* women try to accuse you of misbehaving. In fact, if they do, call me in and I'll give you my support.'

'That's real good of you, ma'am,' the sergeant declared. 'Come on, boys. Let's go take a look.'

From her place of concealment behind the bushes, being able to see and hear everything through the open front door, Calamity was impressed and amused by the performance of the lady outlaw. It was quite a feat for one of her height and far from unnoticeable physical attributes to contrive to look small and helpless in a fashion which aroused the protective instincts of all three burly peace officers and persuaded them to do as she required. She had achieved her purpose and, after the trio entered the dining room, she emerged to hurry along the path.

* * *

'Far be it for me to say I told you so,' Belle Stair commented, having slid down the rope supplied by the hotel as a means of escape in case of fire. 'But I told you there'd be time for me to come here and pick up all my belongings.'

'And I'll bet I *never* hear the last of it,' Calamity Jane replied, holding the carpetbag which had been dropped from the window by the lady outlaw. 'Let's get going.'

Having seen the policemen coming from the other direction and turning through the gates, the driver had brought his hackney cab from where he was waiting further along the street. Leaving the vehicle out of sight, he had kept watch along the path and, because of the debt of gratitude he owed to Dobey Killem and the liking he had formed for Calamity Jane, he had been ready to do whatever he could to help her and her companion escape should this prove necessary. They had got away without any need for intervention on his part and, once they were aboard, he had driven off at a speed suggestive of urgency, but not sufficiently fast to arouse suspicion.

On the way to the hotel, Belle had done what she could to make herself presentable for going inside. Using a towel from the bag she had given to the redhead when explaining her plan for dealing with the feminists, she had dried her face and torso. Then, while Calamity was doing the same with a clean shirt, she had extracted and changed into a blouse similar to the one damaged in the fighting. Asked about her plans now the situation had changed so drastically, she had stated her belief that there would be sufficient time before the suspicions of the sergeant were directed her way for her to collect her property and make good her escape.

Reverting to being "Betty Hardin" and behaving in a flustered and embarrassed manner while retrieving the jewelry she had left in the safe, Belle had informed the desk clerk that she did not wish to be disturbed by Mary Abbott or any other member of the "Women's Rights Movement." Suspecting their sexual proclivities, he had drawn the conclusion she sought to produce and assumed the insistence stemmed from them having tried to force their attentions upon her. Having locked and bolted the door of her room, she had packed the carpetbag. Dropping it to where Calamity was waiting in the alley, she had made her descent without difficulty or being seen by anybody else.

'As if *I'd* boast about *anything*,' Belle said, as she and Calamity set off to where the driver was waiting with his hackney cab.

'But I *did* tell you how Abbott and her kind hate peace officers near as much as they hate us Southrons and wouldn't be wanting to admit to *men*—especially *lawmen*—how a Southron girl took them the way I did. Besides which, even when he found out that I'd gone instead of staying, I reckon the sergeant'd be even more willing to reckon it was them and not Senator Dillwater's niece who brought the forged cash and marked cards into the game.'

'He's going to be riled as a stick-teased rattler when he finds out you're not kin to the Senator,' Calamity guessed.

'Why sure,' the lady outlaw agreed. 'Only, by the time either he or any other of the local law comes looking for "Betty Hardin", she'll be long gone. And I reckon it would be better if you're not around either, Calam.'

'Something told me's I'd likely wind up that way, the company I've been keeping,' the redhead replied, confident that her friend could elude any pursuit given so much of a start. Having anticipated the contingency, she had made arrangements for her safety with the approval of Dobey Killem. 'So I've got my gear packed and a hoss waiting. Should anybody go 'round the outfit and ask, they'll get told I lit out at sundown to see what the trail end towns have to offer, 'cause Topeka's been too danged quiet for me. Which it was afore our trails crossed and'd get that way again once you've gone.'

NOTES:

Although they had not been brought to trial, Mary Abbott and her group feared they would be as a result of the complaints they believed would be lodged when their victims received the promissory notes. Therefore, they fled to the East and, scattering, were never again involved in the feminist campaign. Although the authorities suspected Belle Starr had been "Betty Hardin", it was considered she had done the community a service by getting rid of them and there was no attempt made to prove her implication.

CPSIA information can be obtained
at www.ICGtesting.com
Printed in the USA
LVHW100616201118
597623LV00017B/383/P